Gaming Masculinity

Gaming

MASCU

FANDOM & CULTURE

Katherine Larsen and Paul Booth, series editors

Trolls, Fake Geeks, and the Gendered Battle for Online Culture

MEGAN CONDIS

UNIVERSITY OF IOWA PRESS, IOWA CITY

University of Iowa Press, Iowa City 52242
Copyright © 2018 by the University of Iowa Press
www.uipress.uiowa.edu
Printed in the United States of America
Design by Lindsay Starr

The University of Iowa Press is a member of Green
Press Initiative and is committed to preserving
natural resources.
Printed on acid-free paper

Library of Congress Cataloging-in-Publication Data
Names: Condis, Megan Amber, 1984– author.
Title: Gaming masculinity : trolls, fake geeks,
and the gendered battle for online culture /
Megan Amber Condis.
Description: Iowa City : University of Iowa Press,
[2018] | Series: Fandom & Culture | Includes
bibliographical references. | Description based
on print version record and cip data provided by
publisher; resource not viewed.
Identifiers: lccn 2017039378 (print) | lccn
2017060010 (ebook) | isbn 9781609385668 (ebk) |
isbn 9781609385651 (pbk : acid-free paper)
Subjects: lcsh: Video games—Social aspects. |
Masculinity in popular culture.
Classification: lcc gv1469.34.s52 (ebook) |
lcc gv1469.34.s52 c65 2018 (print) |
ddc 794.8—dc23
lc record available at https://lccn.loc.gov
/2017039378

FOR AMY

CONTENTS

ACKNOWLEDGMENTS

THERE ARE SO MANY PEOPLE who supported me as I went through the process of writing this book that I hardly know where to begin.

Of course I must extend my most sincere thanks to my dissertation committee: Stephanie Foote, Lisa Nakamura, Spencer Schaffner, and J. B. Capino. I cannot express how important their insightful critiques and pointed questions were to me.

I would also like to thank Andrea Stevens, Justine Murison, Renée Trilling, and Sarah Projansky for helping me to position this project (and myself) on the academic job market. Robert Barrett, Gordon Hutner, Melissa Littlefield, Lauri Newcomb, Robert Dale Parker, Curtis Perry, Anthony Pollock, Siobhan Sommerville, Robert Warrior, Charles Wright, Karen Flynn, Chantal Nadeau, Mimi Nguyen, Fiona Ngô, Dianne Harris, Rob Rushing, Sandy Camargo, Lilya Kaganovsky, Cris Mayo, and Isabel Molina-Guzmán provided guidance and encouragement in seminars at the undergraduate and graduate levels. High school teachers like Barb Katz, Elizabeth Rebmann, and Brian Deters inspired me and nurtured my (no doubt annoying) inquisitiveness.

My colleagues at Stephen F. Austin State University have also been of immense help to me. I would particularly like to thank Mark Sanders, Andrew Brininstool, Deborah Bush, Jackie Cowan, Michael Given, Marc Guidry, Ericka Hoagland, Steve Marsden, Michael Martin, Christine McDermott, John McDermott, Laura Osborne, Tom Reynolds, Christopher Sams, Jessica Sams, Michael Sheehan, Elizabeth Tasker Davis, Kenneth Untiedt, Amber Wagnon, Kevin West, and Sue Whatley.

I must thank the participants in the 2013–14 IPRH Fellowship Seminar for their diverse and brilliant insights. I would also like to thank Donald and Barbara Smalley for supporting a fellowship in gender and women's studies that supported me at a crucial time while I was writing this book.

My fellow graduate students were indispensible as intellectual partners and emotional allies. Thank you to Karo Engstrom, T. J. Tallie, Franklin Ridgeway, Derek Attig, Kaitlin Marks-Dubbs, Ben Bascom, Melissa Kaye Forbes, Marthea Webber, Elaine Wood, Amber Buck, Sarah Sahn, Erin Heath, Sarah Alexander Tsai, Amanda Zink, Ashley Hetrick, Shantal Martinez, Stephanie Brown, Mel Stanfill, Lisa Oliverio, Jill Hamilton Clements, Erin Schroyer McQuiston, Alicia Kozma, Ezra Claverie, and Melissa Girard.

Without the council of Jennifer Daly, Lauri Harden, Jennifer Price, Amy Rumsey, Stephanie Shockey, Deborah Stauffer, Rebecca Crain, Gina Ajero, and Jacquelyn Kahn, I would have floundered in university bureaucracies. Thank you for your patience and your assistance in all matters great and small.

My coaches and teammates at CrossFit Trilogy and Central Illinois Combat Club kept me healthy and sane. Thank you to Bob Long, Jeremy Pasley, Ryan Smith, Kelly Madden, Gavin Vansaghi, Wade Choate, Mike Taylor, and Jason Stramberg for teaching me to believe in myself and in the strength of my body and mind. Special thanks to the women of Trilogy—Brook McCreary, Sarah Morris, April Lovell, Jamie Cates, Kelly Davenport, Alli McClanahan, Kristi Bennett, Megan Taylor, Jill LaCost, Jesi Sciortino, Sarah Beal, Brandi Bailey, Stephanie Larson, Morgan Lynn, Liz Dill, Jani Davis, Krista Bontemps, Diana Schmitt, Kambell Bennett, Darcey Drockelman, Jenna Schultz, Angie Fangmeier, and Liz Lewis—for being the best friends anyone could ask for. I am especially grateful to my Sparkle Motion teammates Missy Rummel and Kelly Girardo. I can't imagine better partners in competition and in life.

Thank you to Courtney and Mikell Wooten, who made my transition into the mysterious land of Texas into the greatest, most fulfilling adventure of my life. I will always be there for you both.

And most of all, thank you to my parents, Amy and Bill Davis; my brother, Zack Davis; and my grandparents, Sally and Ron Ferko and Henrietta Davis. Everything I've ever done that was any good was only possible because of you. I love you. Thank you.

Gaming Masculinity

Introduction:
The Gamification of Gender

N 2015, THE PHRASE "social justice warrior" was added to the *Oxford English Dictionary*. Defined as derogatory noun to describe "a person who expresses or promotes socially progressive views," it entered the mainstream after years of use in the gaming subculture, where it was a popular shorthand way to discredit and dismiss anyone who presented views that contradicted the straight white male majority. By 2016, many of the same gamers who popularized that phrase were directing their anger at Zoë Quinn, a female game developer. Gamers mercilessly taunted and harassed Quinn because, they alleged, she traded sexual favors with a journalist in exchange for positive reviews of a short indie game she had created in 2013 called *Depression Quest* (Mother Jones News Team 2014). The allegation was swiftly discredited (Chapter 4), but that didn't stop them from harassing her. Quinn was inundated with rape and death threats. Her home address and personal phone number were distributed online. Her devices were hacked and her personal photos leaked, all supposedly in the name of addressing a breach of ethics in games journalism—even though Quinn was not a journalist. The #GamerGate movement had begun.

Most of us have participated in gaming culture in one form or another, whether playing *Words with Friends* (Zynga, 2009) or *Angry Birds* (Rovio Entertainment, 2009) on our phones, checking our crops in *Farmville* (Zynga, 2009) while browsing Facebook, sneaking in a hand or two of *Solitaire* (Microsoft 3.0, 1990) at work, or gathering around a console to play *Wii Sports* (Nintendo, 2006) or *Rock Band* (Harmonix Music Systems, MTV Games, 2007) at a party. However, most people don't think of themselves as gamers. Gamers are self-identified members of a subcultural group organized around video game fandom. They do not dabble with video games; they *live* video games. They think of gaming as constituting an important part of their identity. And in August 2014, GamerGaters were very unhappy to hear cultural critics claim that gamers were over.

Writers who expressed this sentiment, like Leigh Alexander (2014), Dan Golding (2014), and Casey Johnston (2014), didn't mean that the gaming industry as a whole was in trouble. Rather, they were referring to the death of a particular image of the gamer: the stereotypical adolescent nerdy straight white boy who scoffs at any digital entertainment that isn't hardcore.

But the tenor of the harassment, and the fact that Quinn, along with Anita Sarkeesian, a feminist games critic, were the focus of most of the hate on display, led many to believe that #GamerGate was actually just a boys' club wing of the gaming community taking advantage of an opportunity to vent their misogyny under the cover of a supposedly legitimate cause (Wofford 2014). Media scholar Dan Golding's (2014) response to the controversy was to condemn the online bullies while remaining somewhat sympathetic toward them. After all, he notes, as games created for diverse, casual audiences became more and more popular, "the traditional gamer identity [was] now culturally irrelevant," no longer the "consumer-king" to which an industry would be forced to bow. The loss of the privilege to which they had been accustomed must be painful, he reasoned. Gaming journalist Leigh Alexander (2014) was a little harsher in her condemnation of the fledgling movement, finding that times were changing, with more and more women and minorities entering the gaming subculture as developers and writers: "We are refusing to let anyone feel prohibited from participating." She also sounded the death knell for the term that had come to define the subculture: "'Gamer' isn't just a dated demographic label that most people increasingly prefer not to use. Gamers are over. That's why they're so mad."

#GamerGate's response was an explosion of vitriol that persisted beyond the Quinn incident. They expanded their list of targets to include prominent female writers as well as their progressive male allies, all of whom were sardonically dismissed as social justice warriors (SJWs), liberal ideologues who want to impose their politically correct politics on gaming culture and who must be stopped at any cost.

At its base, #GamerGate was an exaggeration of the normative rhetorical practices of hardcore online gamers, a blown-up version of their complex and contradictory views regarding the politics of embodiment and identity. In turn, the reactionary politics of gamers are an extension of the backlash politics of the American right wing, the politics of the aggrieved straight white man who wants to build a wall to keep out immigrants and thinks that feminists are causing the "wussification" of our culture (McDonough 2014). By mapping the various contours and contradictions within gamer culture, we can create a miniature model of how we understand gender, sexuality, and race, and we can track how these concepts are stretched and reshaped to fit various subcultural contexts. We see familiar power dynamics at work in gamer culture; however, occasionally they wind up so warped as to become vulnerable. It is in these spaces of tension and flexibility, where hierarchy meets anarchy on the virtual playing fields of online gaming culture, that the idea of what it means to be a man in our day and age is being defined anew.

In this book, I examine how gender politics are being filtered through and produced by the logic of video games. I illustrate some of the game-like principles that operate in our expressions of gender, both online and off. Of course, the timeliness of such an examination is clear, as the video game industry is currently "one of the fastest growing sectors in the US economy" ("Game Player Data" 2013); it is "more than twice the size of the recorded-music industry, nearly a quarter more than the magazine business and about three-fifths the size of the film industry, counting DVD sales as well as box-office receipts" ("All the World's a Game" 2011). Moreover, many other industries are looking to digital gamification to create new tools for interacting with customers, driving research and development, and training employees. For example, tech entrepreneur David Edery and business scholar Ethan Mollick describe how video games are used to market new products, gather data about potential customers, and commodify the labor of loyal fans. Byron Reeves and J. Leighton Reed (2009) write about how businesses can use games to improve their hiring practices, facilitate cooperation, and drive worker productivity. Meanwhile, linguist

James Paul Gee (2007) and digital media scholar Kurt Squire (2011) advocate for the use of video games and virtual worlds in the classroom, and writer/artist Mary Flanagan (2009) and scholar/game designer Ian Bogost (2007) describe how games can be used by activists and politicians to persuade audiences and motivate them to take action for a particular cause. Game designer Jane McGonigal (2008) and communication studies scholar Daren C. Brabham (2014) imagine a future when the collective intelligence of gamers might be used to solve complex problems, as when, for example, players of the online game *Foldit* (University of Washington, 2008; the game has been described as being like *Tetris* [Alexey Pajitnov, Nintendo, 1989] on steroids) were able to figure out "the structure of an enzyme that AIDS-like viruses use for reproduction," a puzzle that "has baffled scientists for more than a decade" (Husted 2011).[1] In a culture that is increasingly saturated in the language and logics of gaming, a culture that is beginning to put the power of gaming to work on a diverse set of problems, we might ask ourselves the following questions: What new insights might be gained by imagining gender itself as a kind of massively multiplayer online (and off-line) role-playing game, one featuring both cooperative and competitive modes, one that is constantly updated and patched to remain popular and relevant? What kinds of gendered expectations are built into the gamelike experiences that we are encountering at work, at school, and in our leisure time? And how might the gamified logics of gender be hacked or exploited by those players who are frustrated with the status quo?

Gender, Performativity, and Play

In 1990 gender theorist Judith Butler explored the subcultural practices of drag performers to illustrate an important truth about how gender works in the broader culture. Butler argues that gender is not a natural biological property of the body but rather exists as a set of "acts, gestures, and desire[s]" that "produce the effect of an internal core or substance . . . on the surface of the body" (2007, 185). She continues, "Such acts, gestures, enactments, generally construed, are performative in the sense that the essence or identity that they otherwise purport to express are fabrications manufactured and sustained through corporeal signs and other discursive means" (186). In other words, according to Butler, gender is something that we do, not something that we are.

Drag performers make the constructed nature of all gendered performances in our day-to-day lives visible by exaggerating, and thus highlight-
ing, their constructedness. They expose the work that it takes to project a
gendered identity, and they revel in the supposed contradictions of their
embodied presentations:

> In imitating gender, drag implicitly reveals the imitative structure of
> gender itself—as well as its contingency. Indeed, part of the pleasure
> the giddiness of the performance is in the recognition of a radical con-
> tingency in the relation between sex and gender in the face of cul-
> tural configurations of causal unities that are regularly assumed to be
> natural and necessary. In the place of the law of heterosexual coher-
> ence, we see sex and gender denaturalized by means of a performance
> which avows their distinctness and dramatizes the cultural mechanism
> of their fabricated unity. (Butler 2007, 187–88)

Drag performers are playing with the rules of gender, and their play provides us with an insight into how masculinity and femininity are defined in
mainstream culture.

Participants in the gaming subculture make a similar move, but it is
in the opposite direction. Gamers look for games in every system they encounter, including systems of gender and sexuality and the various hierarchies of power built thereon. Thus, the field of gendered and sexualized
(and racialized and classed) identities becomes one of many playing fields,
a space to be inhabited strategically. For gamers, gender identity is a contest that can be won. This is the philosophy of identity that is spilling over
into mainstream culture and politics as gaming becomes more integrated
into our everyday lives.

This argument runs counter to the views of many early adopters of
Internet technology, who at first predicted that the advent of virtual worlds
such as those found in video games and massively multiplayer online role-
playing games (MMORPGs) would mark the end of gender, and even of the
body, as we know it. These technoutopians, to use Turner's (2008) term,
argued that as more and more of our daily lives took place online rather
than in person, the importance of embodiment as a marker of identity (and
thus the various forms of discrimination that have arisen around embodied
differences) would fade away, leaving a pure, objective meritocracy in its

wake. Online, people would be judged according to their helpfulness, intelligence, personality, and their character, and not the color of their skin or the configuration of their genitals.

The cyber dreams of the technoutopians are framed as "meat-free dreams"—so much so that "cyberculture's aficionados often appear to have forgotten that they have bodies at all" (Adam 2002, 159). As posthumanist scholar Allucquére Roseanne Stone puts it, "The discourse of visionary virtual world builders is rife with images of imaginal bodies freed from the constraints that flesh imposes. Cyberspace developers foresee a time when they will be able to forget about the body" (2000, 525). This claim is usually couched in hopeful terms as they attempt to explain how the new social order created online will be free of the scourges of racism, sexism, homophobia, and ableism.

In the mid- to late 1990s, technoutopian rhetoric sang the praises of the disembodied web. "A Declaration of the Independence of Cyberspace" contains a passage outlining the positive political consequences that are assumed to follow from the creation of a society without bodies:

> We are creating a world that all may enter without privilege or prejudice accorded by race, economic power, military force, or station of birth. . . .
>
> Our identities have no bodies, so, unlike you, we cannot obtain order by physical coercion. We believe that from ethics, enlightened self-interest, and the commonweal, our governance will emerge. Our identities may be distributed across many of your jurisdictions. The only law that all our constituent cultures would generally recognize is the Golden Rule. (Barlow 1996)

Academic and cultural critic Howard Rheingold also praised the web as an equal opportunity environment, noting that on the Internet,

> race, gender, age, national origin, and physical appearance are not apparent unless a person wants to make such characteristics public. . . . People whose physical handicaps make it difficult to form new friendships find that virtual communities treat them as they always wanted to be treated—as thinkers and transmitters of idea and feeling beings, not carnal vessels with a certain appearance and way of walking and talking (or not walking and talking). (1993, 26)

According to this logic, the primary draw of virtual reality is the power that it gives users to discard their bodies altogether. This will level the playing field of social interaction, the thinking goes, as discrimination on the basis of bodily traits will be impossible when users are unable to see those with whom they are interacting.

Other optimistic early adopters took a different approach, instead emphasizing the possibilities of the Internet as a space of free play, a space where categories like gender and race cease to become vectors for the distribution of power and resources. Instead, the categories will be reborn as the harmless stuff of postmodern identity pastiche. In a virtual world where we can craft any type of appearance we like (and as many different appearances as we like), these theorists posited, gender and race could exist free of cultural baggage and function purely as modes of individual expression. For example, Sherry Turkle posits that "the Internet has become a significant social laboratory for experimenting with the constructions and reconstructions of self that characterize postmodern life. In its virtual reality, we self-fashion and self-create" (1995, 180). She discusses the possibilities afforded by virtual gender swapping and for the creation of new genders and null genders, which, she argues, "serve as a form of consciousness-raising about gender issues" (214) by enabling a new dialogue around the subject of identity and self-presentation, as well as the establishment of social and political norms in the new communities being formed online. In a similar vein, Lisa Nakamura describes how ordinary users, role players in the earliest text-based multiuser MUDs and MOOs[2] thought of racial identity as "a matter of aesthetics, or finding the color that you like, rather than as a matter of ethnic identity or shared cultural referents. This fantasy of skin color divorced from politics, oppression, or racism seems to also celebrate it as infinitely changeable and customizeable: as entirely elective as well as apolitical" (2002, 53). According to this logic, race and gender are emptied of any broader cultural significance. They are transformed into mere accessories that can be tried on for awhile, then removed once they become tiresome.

Unfortunately, as anyone who has spent much time reading comments on *YouTube* videos, waiting in *Call of Duty* (Infinity Ward, Activision, 2003) pregame lobbies, or spending time in the *League of Legends* (Riot Games, 2009) ranked solo queue knows, these utopian dreams have not yet come to pass. We have not come to disregard our bodies; nor have we transformed them into accessories. Instead we imported them into the digital landscape, reducing the brave new world of the Internet into one resembling the familiar old one. In part this development reflects the politics of the era in which Internet use first became popular among nonspecialist users. Nakamura (2008) notes that the early 1990s was a time when the rise of neoliberal politics and postfeminist discourse had a chilling effect on discussions of social justice around issues of race and gender. As with other neoliberal systems, the veil of hoped-for meritocracy promised by a meat-free Internet actually resulted in the privileging of white male middle-class subjects over all others. The supposedly bodiless dwellers of the utopian Internet came to be read as straight white men by default. Thus, those who experienced racial or gendered discrimination online were blamed for their own abuse. After all, if they didn't want to be harassed, they could simply choose to pass as a member of the dominant class. By outing themselves as female or black or queer online, they were said to invite oppression by inviting the unwelcome body back into the online space.

However, as ideologies of gender and race were interpreted and deployed in the subcultural communities organized around the Internet and online gaming, their adaptation into these new formats was not always perfect. As they warped and shifted according to the tenets of the virtual worlds inhabited by gamers, new cracks opened up within gendered and racialized discourses that may in turn create an opportunity for new insights into the nature of the game of gender. Over the course of this book, I will explore how gamers came to understand embodied identity online in both expected and unexpected ways through the logics of gaming.

In our increasingly networked world, it is useful to think of gender as an MMORPG, like the popular *World of Warcraft* (Blizzard Entertainment, 2004). In this kind of system, information is just as important as our bodies (if not more so), and we alternate between collaborating and competing with each other to achieve a constantly shifting set of goals. Unlike most video games, MMORPGs do not have an ending. They cannot be beaten. Instead, they ask players to grind—to repeat the same gestures and the same quests over and over, in hopes of receiving a rare piece of treasure they can show off to others. Similarly, gender is never something that can be finished. There is no threshold beyond which a gendered identity is thoroughly and irrevocably established. Instead, we must tend to our identities daily, repeatedly evoking the same rituals in exchange for intermittent social rewards.

Two important game design terms are crucial to understanding how gender functions in this subculture: game mechanics and emergent dynamics. Game mechanics are the types of moves available to the player that are discovered over the course of play, like jumping in *Super Mario Bros.* (Nintendo, 1985) or throwing a Hadoken fireball in *Street Fighter* (Capcom, 1987). Emergent dynamics, on the other hand, might take weeks, months, or even years to be discovered. They are the accidental, unpredicted behaviors that a game allows in addition or even in spite of the intentions of the designer.

Chapters 1 and 2 describe two commonly used game mechanics in the game of gender. Chapter 1 examines trolling, a game of emotional manipulation in which the winner is the one who can maintain an air of cool rationality in the face of provocation. Both the form and the content of this game are organized around gendered tropes, making trolling a kind of masculinity contest. Chapter 2 looks at the Internet memes that circulate around femininity in the gaming world. Participating in meme culture is like decoding a language puzzle or playing a riddle game. Players demonstrate that they are in the know by constructing messages that adhere to the rules and codes of the subculture in which they are embedded. These memes help gamers who are invested in the masculine dominance of online spaces to make sense of the ever-growing population of female gamers by recasting them as feminine stereotypes like the inexperienced novice, the nurturing support, or the castrating whore.

In these chapters, I demonstrate that despite the supposedly disembodied nature of life online, performances of masculinity are still afforded privileged status in gamer culture. Gamers are expected to conform or pass as stylized masculine subjects (via textual performances) or face the consequence of social ostracization. However, because the porting[3] of stereotypical masculine tropes from the context of the physical world into the context of a virtual world is not and can never be perfect, women and queer gamers are increasingly finding effective emergent game dynamics in the game of gender. Emergent game dynamics are strategies, tactics, and practices that game developers didn't originally anticipate when they were building the game but that emerged organically from the player community. Often these practices enable players to take a game in entirely new and unplanned directions. Occasionally, as in the case of hacks and exploits, they enable gamers to break the game—that is, engage in a kind of play that circumvents the game's challenges or enables them to sidestep certain obstacles. Both Chapters 2 and 3 look at some of the emergent game dynamics that are popping up in the online game of gender.

In Chapter 2, for example, I look at examples of countermemes created to talk back to the dominant strain of gender discourse within gamer culture while simultaneously signaling the in-group status of the meme's creator. By mobilizing recognizable subcultural tropes, users signal their authenticity and their knowledge of the social norms of their group even as they challenge them. In Chapter 3, I look at how female and queer gamers are turning on its head the assumption that AAA video games can only be profitable if they appeal exclusively to a straight white adolescent male demographic by demanding representation in games like *Mass Effect* (BioWare, 2007), *Dragon Age* (BioWare, 2009), and *Star Wars: The Old Republic* (BioWare, Electronic Arts, Lucas Arts, 2011). These gamers are organizing and collaborating; they are hacking the cultural code of gendered performance. Their example suggests that even the most pervasive, most long-lived, most deeply engrained ideologies can be cracked through a combination of flexible tactics and collective action.

Finally, in Chapter 4 and the Epilogue, I look at how the logics of gaming are making their way into other arenas. From presidential politics to online dating, gaming culture provides participants with potent metaphors to model complex social arrangements. Chapter 4 tackles #GamerGate and its synergistic relationship with the alt-right and the then–2016 Republican presidential candidate Donald Trump. In the Epilogue, I consider the gamified design of social media dating apps like Tinder, and I encourage designers and those who work in the tech industry to think about how the various types of gamification that we encounter across all aspects of life might have, purposefully or not, been developed in ways that are marked by gender. This is an important task for the digital humanities as a field of inquiry; in addition to developing new hardware and software for our own use (including the creation of educational digital games), we need to provide our own critiques of those tools. We need to pay attention to how they are made, as well as by whom and for whom. We need to ask ourselves if, in the rush to gamify our world, we might be accidentally excluding some from the brave new (virtual) worlds we are creating. .

Game Break

Bro's Law

ARMY OF TWO AND THE PERILS OF
PARODY IN GAMING CULTURE

Kaceytron is a satirical character, a kind of Stephen Colbert of the gaming world. Her persona is a mix of annoying characteristics designed to drive people, particularly gamers, crazy. For example, she calls herself a "professional girl gamer" (Kaceytron 2014), yet she often plays extremely poorly. Her broadcasts consist mostly of her bragging about her abilities, denigrating her teammates, and screaming obscenities at her viewers. In short, she is an intentionally unpleasant character. Part of her shtick involves putting her body on display in the stream. This often causes viewers to angrily call her a cam whore and berate her for using sex appeal instead of gaming skill to earn donations from fans. Is she intentionally using her sexuality to drive donations? Or is she mockingly embodying the stereotype of what some sexist gamers think women's streams are all like?

Kaceytron's performance is a kind of "long form improv" (MostlyBiscuit 2015) that takes place on her video stream on *Twitch.tv*, and her show entertains thousands of fans for several hours a day, four or five days a week. In return, she receives money from ad revenue and donations from her audi-

ence. While most of the popular streamers on *Twitch.tv* gain a following because they are excellent players (many are professional e-sports athletes) or
because they are well liked by their community, Kaceytron is seemingly famous for being one of, if not the most, controversial individuals on the site.
As a result, many of her viewers apparently take pleasure in hate-watching
her stream, making small donations just so that she will read their abusive
and hateful messages about her out loud (pleaseTWITCHdontMUTEem
2014).

Some of the most controversial parts of her act involve her satirizing
many of the gendered stereotypes that abound in gaming culture. In an
out-of-character interview with *Femhype*, Kaceytron remarks, " People who
look at the character I portray on stream and are unable to detect the sar-
casm in it and take it a step further by assuming *all* female gamers are like
that, I think truly [there] are very few . . . and the ones that do exist are obviously of low intelligence and not worth my time" (MostlyBiscuit 2015). However, it looks as though there are a lot more gamers out there than Kaceytron realizes who aren't in on the joke. Threads with titles like "Is Kaceytron
for real or not?" (Taiso 2015) and "Is Kaceytron trolling?" (nerdonator 2013)
pop up in gaming forums all over the web. Sometimes viewers will take it
upon themselves to out her as a fraud once they discover that she is only
playacting (fimontronia 2014).

At the same time, Kaceytron's most dedicated fans love both her over-
the-top persona and the various meltdowns that she inspires in the unini-
tiated. They claim to be in on the joke. But for my part, the more I watched
her interact with her fans in the stream, the more uncomfortable I became.
I began to wonder if part of the true appeal of the stream was that it gave
viewers a license to partake in misogynist discourse under the protection
of its being ironic or just a part of the show.[1] How can we explain this phenomenon and ones like it, where it becomes difficult to separate the trolls
from the trolled, the critiques of sexism from expressions of it?

I propose a new Internet maxim that I will call Bro's Law, a corollary
to the famous Poe's Law, which describes the inherent difficulty in sepa-
rating out actual, sincere statements of extremist views from parodies of
those same views. The original formulation of Poe's Law states that "without a winking smiley or other blatant display of humor, it is utterly impossible to parody a Creationist in such a way that *someone* won't mistake [it]
for the genuine article" (Poe 2015). It was coined by Nathan Poe in a discussion about religion, and it highlights the difficulty of coming up with exag-

gerated versions of an already extreme discourse. In his discussion of Poe's Law, Scott F. Aikin remarks, "The humor and point of these sorts of parody is to present religious bigotry and scientific illiteracy in a fashion that magnifies it and thereby highlights its vice. The question, though, is how *magnified* those parodies really are. Even the most casual websurfing yields similar, if not *more* shocking scientific illiteracy and religious bigotry" (2013, 303). In popular usage, Poe's Law has been evoked to describe extreme political positions of all kinds, not just of religious origin (Aikin 2013, 302). Those who evoke Poe's Law imply that some philosophical systems are sufficiently ridiculous that the sincerely offered statements of belief offered by those within that system will appear to be a parody to those on the outside. At the same time, Poe's Law suggests that it will be difficult for those within the belief system to tell whether a new entrant into the conversation is legitimately a believer or simply a troll posing as one.

Bro's Law functions similarly. It states:

Without a winking smiley or other blatant display of humor (and sometimes even with one), it is utterly impossible to parody the views about gender held by many in gaming culture in such a way that someone won't mistake it for the genuine article.

For example, Kaceytron's larger-than-life performance of a fake geek girl persona is apparently mistaken by many to be the sincere performance of a woman intruding into the heretofore masculine space of online gaming culture. At the same time, it is difficult to tell which of the hateful, misogynist comments that accompany her donations are sincerely hateful and which are a kind of audience participation with her performance by fans who enjoy her schtick.

Bro's Law can also be applied to content within games, as in the celebratory "bro-downs" in *Army of Two* (Electronic Arts, 2008). As the title suggests, the game is best experienced in cooperative mode: two players work together strategically to make it through each area alive. For example, a teammate can lay down suppressive fire to draw attention away from the partner, or can boost the partner onto a ledge to gain higher ground. While the game's subject matter has the potential to reflect seriously on post-9/11 geopolitical affairs such as the use of private military contractors in the war on terror, the tone of the game is silly. Some of the game's most memorable moments arise from the "show appreciation" feature: "Walk up to your partner and press 'A,'" the tutorial instructs us, "to show enthusiasm for something your partner has done." Doing so causes the two player characters to perform a brief bro-tastic animation, including high fives, fist bumps, air guitar, and frat boy—esque turns of phrase like "Big ups, yo!" "Props, bro," and even, "Ladies, lift your shirts!" Are these animations meant to be ridiculous, despite the seriousness of the plot involving assassinations and killers for hire? Or are they sincerely meant to be cool? Are they attempts to alleviate the gay panic that a game built around the concept of the close partnership of a pair of masked, burly military men who have each other's backs might evoke? (The signature pose of the game's two playable avatars has them standing back to back.) Or are they making fun of such ubermasculine displays by intentionally protesting too much? All these seemingly contradictory interpretations are equally plausible because the extreme performances of masculinity we've seen in other games throughout gaming history are so wild that it is not out of the question to suggest that this is simply one in a long line of such portrayals.

Case studies for Bro's Law can also be found in the corporate world, where the excesses of the so-called brogrammer culture can be alienating to women interested in entering careers in tech. Take the presentation of the Titstare app, where "you take photos of yourself staring at tits" at TechCrunch Disrupt 2013 (Morias 2013), or the career fair materials inviting potential employees to "bro down and crush code" for the social media analytics company Klout (Raja 2012). Some argue that these examples were nothing more than satirical jokes aimed at skewering the boys-only vibe at many tech companies. But whether these incidents were intentionally exclusionary, unintentionally offensive, or self-aware and poking fun at sexist attitudes, they are difficult to read correctly against the backdrop of sexism that permeates every aspect of tech culture. Bro's Law suggests that the effects these statements have on actual women working and participating in gaming are real, regardless of whether the sentiments behind them are sincere.

1

"Get Raped, F****t"

TROLLING AS A GENDERED METAGAME

ONLINE SPACES DEVOTED TO GAMER CULTURE are filled with subcultural codes of conduct designed to police expressions of masculinity. Gamers monitor their own behavior as well as that of their friends by affecting disdain for anything that could be considered feminine or gay. They enact what C. J. Pascoe calls the "repeated repudiation of the specter of failed masculinity" (2007, 5) lest they be ostracized from the group. Part of this work involves repeatedly proclaiming one's heterosexuality through the production of homophobic discourse. Gamers thus regularly "lay claim to masculine identities by lobbing homophobic epithets at one another" (5). This is plain to anyone who has spent time in gaming circles and listened to the insults being flung during play. However, these exchanges are more than merely an unpleasant side effect of gaming's competitive atmosphere. Some gamers frequently turn masculine policing into a metagame in its own right, a game in which one improves one's own standing both by enacting masculine performances of dominance and self-mastery, and by successfully baiting others into losing status by letting their mask of masculinity slip. The result is a singular set of performative gender codes that is unique to this corner of the Internet.

The primary game mechanic in this gendered metagame is commonly known as trolling, or the posting of "inflammatory, extraneous, or off-topic messages in an online community, such as an online discussion forum, chat room, or blog, with the primary intent of provoking other users into a desired emotional response or of otherwise disrupting normal on-topic discussion" (Cambria et al. 2010). In the spaces frequented by participants in the video game subculture, trolling is an exercise in ascribing gender to oneself and to others. For example, trolls will attempt to solicit responses from their victims using gendered taunts ("bitch," "fag") and by alluding to rape and domestic violence as a metaphor for their dominance in a game. In addition, female gamers, developers, and feminist-identified video game critics are often selected as targets for troll or hacker attacks.

Yet trolling in the video game community goes beyond the simple use of sexist rhetoric. On a fundamental level, trolling is a gendered discursive act, no matter what kind of language the troll uses to cause offense and no matter what population the troll targets. The game of trolling sorts participants into two camps. One camp comprises those who refuse to take the bait. They demonstrate a cool-headed rationality, a mastery over the self that is traditionally associated with the performance of masculinity. The other camp comprises those who take the bait and feed the troll. They are imagined as overly earnest and emotional, as feminine. In other words, the game is set up to reinforce the idea that competent Internet users and elite gamers are defined precisely as those who enact a masculine textual performance (no matter the sex of their actual body) while the chumps and newbs[1] of the gaming world are those who are unable to maintain a masculine facade under pressure. In a digital environment where the body on the other side of the screen is unknowable, policing mechanisms like trolling are well suited to the purpose of gendered discipline because they work by rhetorical posturing. Gamers need not prove that they have a male body to win at the game of trolling. They need only acquiesce to the proposition that a masculine textual presentation (a writing style that values traditionally masculine traits and dismisses all things feminine as undesirable) is the key to earning respect in the gaming community. Of course, not all gamers are active trolls. However, the normalization and widespread acceptance of the presence of trolls in the community and on the Internet at large create a chilling effect on female participation in the culture by positing that gendered abuse is to be expected in gaming culture, and that expressions of outrage about such abuse are nothing more than a sign of naïveté and inexperience.

Again, this does not mean that all trolls are necessarily men or that their victims are necessarily women.[2] Because trolling takes place online, it is impossible to tell who the trolls really are, demographically or biologically. Further, trolls who disclose information about their supposed race, gender, and age can hardly be trusted. As Whitney Phillips (2013) explains, their claims to particular identities might simply be a part of the construction of their troll persona. Rather, it means that both the form of trolling (the rules of the rhetorical game) and its content (gendered insults, references to gendered acts of violence) encourage participants to conform to a writing style that aligns with what our culture thinks of as masculine and to disdain and denigrate styles marked as feminine. Thus, a woman who successfully trolls someone raises her status in the troll community by pulling off a masculine performance of aloofness, while a man who falls for a troll's bait exposes himself, at least in that moment, as unacceptably feminine by indulging in an emotional outburst. It might be impossible to tell if a poster is a woman, but the game of trolling allows participants to imagine that they can tell when a poster is acting womanly, and it incentivizes players to avoid behaviors that might be seen as such lest they lose face.

This set of discursive rules makes it difficult for in-group members to articulate, or even conceptualize, dissention. According to trolling logic, membership in the community means that (and is measured by the fact that) one has the same unemotional masculine-coded reaction to provoking and sexist statements as everyone else. There is little space for disagreement over the codes that govern group membership because group membership only becomes visible through conformity to those codes. One can either roll with the trolls or risk being targeted by them. Thus, trolling works as a silencing disciplinary mechanism on the wider community. Those who disagree with trolling tactics but still consider themselves gamers are incentivized to keep quiet about it lest they be singled out as outsiders themselves.

Trolling 101

WHAT IS A TROLL?

According to Susan Herring et al., the term "troll" originally referred to "the practice used in fishing where a baited line is dragged behind a boat, although some Internet discourse refers to the troll as a fictional monster waiting under the bridge to snare innocent bystanders" (2002, 372). Its association with high-profile antibullying and online harassment campaigns has led some scholars like Jonathan Bishop (2012) to claim that the word is becoming overused. Indeed, Farhad Manjoo (2012) argues that the term has become so watered down in common usage that it is now nothing more than "a name given to someone who disagrees with you on the Internet," an ad hominem attack used to dismiss or discredit anyone who goes against the majority opinion in a given space. However, by comparing academic definitions of trolling with definitions created by self-professed trolls, I hope to arrive at a working definition of the term that distinguishes true trolls—the agents of chaos who think of themselves as playing a game— from merely disagreeable people.

Archetypal trolls go about their unpleasant and disruptive activities using a unique methodology. Claire Hardaker (2010, 218) argues that trolling is not exactly the same thing as purposeful rudeness (which is meant to be understood by the recipient as a slight or an attack) or as an accidental faux pas (which is simply an etiquette mistake on the part of the communicator and not an intended provocation). Rather, trolling is a complex communicative act that simultaneously targets two audiences: the victim, who must be convinced that the troll's inflammatory statement is sincere and thus is in need of rebuke, and one's fellow trolls, who must be able to recognize the actual intended purpose of the post, which is to generate "bites," or "sincere, responses . . . such as anger, shock, and curiosity . . . in other words, a demonstration by the respondent that he had unwittingly been deceived by the troller's professed pseudo-intent, and was unaware of her *real* intent" (Hardaker 2010, 233). Michele Tepper writes,

> When it takes place within a single, closed community, trolling can sometimes be accepted and reinforced in the . . . subculture because it serves the dual purpose of enforcing community standards and of increasing community cohesion by providing a game that all those who know the rules can play against those who do not. It works both as a game and as a method of subcultural boundary demarcation because the playing pieces in this game are not plastic markers or toy money but pieces of information. (1997, 40)

Trolling becomes a mechanism within subcultural communities that is used to distinguish between longtime, loyal gamers and newbies, inexperienced users who have yet to pay their dues and earn the respect of their fellows. After all, "if no one can be prevented from reading or writing to the group" or from participating in an online game, then "there must be some way of distinguishing between those posters to the group who are actually 'in' the group and those who are still 'outside' it, and all this must be accomplished through asynchronous textual production, with none of the verbal or visual cues that are so crucial to traditional notions of subcultural formation" (45). Tepper describes "the hoped for response" by a troll from a newbie as "an indignant correction":

> It is through such a correction that the complicated play of cultural capital that constitutes trolling begins. The corrector, being outside of the community in which trolling is practiced, believes he is proving his superiority to the troller by catching the troller's error, but he is in fact proving his inferior command of the codes of the local subculture in which trolling is practiced. (41)

Interestingly, throughout Tepper's text, she describes both the troll and the trolling victim as male. Whether she intended this or not, her account reinforces the twin notions that the Internet is a predominantly masculine space and that trolling is a contest of masculine performance.

Trolls originating in one online community also sometimes join together to strike out at other communities, thus defining themselves in opposition to the group they have targeted (Herring et al. 2002). Such trolls might post disruptive comments designed to throw the targeted community into chaos, or they might simply hack into their target's website in an attempt to shut the community down. These incursions serve the dual purpose of infuriating the target and boosting the social capital of the troll.

Surveillance, Discipline, and Power

GAMER SLANG AND MASCULINE ANXIETY

Those who want to be acknowledged as a member of a subcultural group have to prove that they can speak the lingo—that they understand the slang, rhetorical tics, common references, and inside jokes that define that group. The slang that defines gamer culture contributes to a rhetorical system in which the performance of masculinity (and the rejection of femininity and queerness) is one of the ways one sutures oneself into the community. It is not enough for one to simply feel sufficiently manly or to identify with positive examples of masculinity. One must continually and vocally reassert one's masculinity to others by rejecting that which is considered insufficiently manly.

The roots of Internet culture, which are steeped in what T. L. Taylor (2012) calls geek masculinity, suggest that the game of trolling developed as a way for those male subjects who found themselves locked out of the privileges associated with successful performances of traditional masculinity in the physical world (because of their failure to achieve certain masculine markers such as bodily strength and athleticism) to (re)claim a new kind of manhood. As Taylor argues, "while computer gamers have been historically conflated with the technically savvy . . . their identity (as with geeks writ large) is also typically framed in opposition to traditional athletic masculinity" (114). For many years, the geek and the nerd were held up as images of failed masculinity to be avoided at all costs. They were often coded as victims of some kind of affliction or disability. Geeks wore glasses. They had braces on their teeth and corrective footwear on their feet. They were either too fat, too skinny, or too weak to be skilled in athletics. They were clumsy and accident prone, sexually inadequate, and socially and emotionally underdeveloped. "Measured against hegemonic masculinity . . . these guys would be found wanting" (117). In fact, according to Mel Stanfill (2010), geeks have traditionally been portrayed in popular media as being so infatuated with their favorite movies, comics, television shows, and video games that they are precluded from having sexual relations with women. Geeks and gamers often found themselves positioned as the insufficiently manly subjects against which the hunky, athletic style of masculinity was measured.

We can thus read the development of technology-based games like hacking and trolling (and video gaming in general) as a means of reconstructing manliness to mean the mastery of technology as opposed to the body, and the ability to dominate in textual or intellectual games as opposed to athletics. Films like *Real Genius* (1985), *Revenge of the Nerds* (1984), *Weird Science* (1985), and *TRON* (1982), as well as books like Ernest Cline's *Ready Player One* (2011), recuperate the male geek by constructing a social space where he can beat the villain (typically a representative of the traditional mold of masculinity, like a popular jock, or a rich, powerful authority figure, like a military man or a CEO), get the girl, and rise to the top of a new hierarchy of masculinity. In these narratives, gaming, hacking, and trolling function as new sports that value quick-wittedness and technological prowess over brute strength. Indeed, the rise of e-sports and the way in which they mimic traditional sports franchises like the NFL and the NBA can be read as an attempt to take on the mantle of masculinity and athletic celebrity but adapt it to a more geek-friendly context (see Taylor 2012).

One textual game commonly played by trolls is what C. J. Pascoe calls fag talk:

> Fag talk and fag imitations serve as a discourse with which boys discipline themselves and each other through joking relationships. Any boy can temporarily become a fag in a given social space or interaction. This does not mean that boys who identify as or are perceived to be homosexual aren't subject to intense harassment. Many are. But becoming a fag has as much to do with failing at the masculine tasks of competence, heterosexual prowess, and strength or in any way revealing weakness or femininity as it does with a sexual identity. This fluidity of the fag identity is what makes the specter of the fag such a powerful disciplinary mechanism. It is fluid enough that boys police their behaviors out of fear of having the fag identity permanently adhere and definitively enough so that boys recognize a fag behavior and strive to avoid it. (2007, 54)

One might be labeled a fag for any number of reasons that may or may not be related to sexual preference. Almost anything can become an occasion for suspicion and the definitions of what constitutes fag behavior are maddenly (intentionally?) vague: "He walks a certain way, talks a certain way, acts a certain way. He's well dressed, sensitive, and emotionally expressive. He has certain tastes in art and music—indeed he has *any* taste in art and music!" (49). As a result, young men must constantly be on their guard; they must constantly monitor the way they present themselves in order to excise any quirks that might be perceived as gay before they are spotted by someone else. Fag talk is constantly circulating, landing temporarily on almost every cultural participant, each of whom must then foist the label off onto someone else to restore status. Like a game of tag, all players occasionally take a turn at being "it." However, the most skilled players are the ones who can avoid being "it" the majority of the time or who can pass the role off to someone else quickly.

Pascoe also uses the language of games to describe masculine performances centered around the rhetorical figure of the faggot: "In this way the fag became a hot potato that no boy wanted to be left holding. One of the best ways to move out of the fag position was to thrust another boy into that position" (2007, 61). Fag talk is not necessarily or even primarily directed toward actual GLBTQ kids; nor is it typically directed at girls. Rather, straight boys direct the threat of faggotry at each other. Pascoe notes that "most boys engaged in these sorts of practices only when in groups" of other boys. "When not in groups—when in one-on-one interactions with boys or girls—boys were much less likely to engage in gendered and sexed dominance practices. In this sense boys became masculine in groups. . . . When with other boys, they postured and bragged" (2007, 107).

Trolls in gaming culture deploy fag talk, including gendered and sexualized insults, in a wide variety of situations. For example, Elena Bertozzi writes that, for gamers, "cultural norms are often reflected in banter, jokes, idiom and insults. . . . When males play in groups, gendered terms such as 'sissy,' 'pussy' and 'fag,' are used as normal and acceptable putdowns. . . . In digital game play, male conversational exchanges often emphasize the establishment of maleness through choice of language and the explicit enunciation of heterosexist norms" (2008, 478). In 2006, a survey conducted with the approval of the University of Illinois bore out Bertozzi's observations. Jason Rockwood found that

> when asked what forms of homophobia people have seen in the gaming community, here are some of what the surveyed said:
>   87.7%—Players use the phrase, "That's so gay."
>   83.4%—Players use the words "gay" or "queer" as derogatory names
>   When asked how frequently players experience homophobia, those surveyed who responded "Always" or "Frequently" equaled 42%. Add in "Sometimes" and it brings up that total to 74.5%.
>   When asked how often those players respond to the homophobia they witness—50.9% total responded "Never" or "Rarely." (Cole 2009)

More than 60 percent of respondents believed the gaming community was either "Somewhat Hostile" or "Very Hostile" to gay and lesbian participants (Sliwinski 2009).

Compulsive Heterosexuality and the Gaming Industry

In addition to disciplinary fag talk, Pascoe identifies "compulsive hetero-sexuality"—a play on Adrienne Rich's (1980) concept of "compulsory heterosexuality"—via "ritualized demonstrations of mastery over girls' bodies" (Pascoe 2007, 23) as an important component of the performance of teenage masculinity. Once again, this performance takes place in the realm of discourse: stories, real or imagined, about sexual escapades and affectations of coolness encapsulated by phrases like "bros before hoes." Like fag talk, discourses of compulsive heterosexuality use women and girls as their instrumental objects but are primarily directed toward other boys. The "sexual bravado" (85) they display is not an expression of desire or lust but a demonstration of power (10) measured in comparison to the rhetorical expressions of sexual dominance made by one's male friends and rivals—or perhaps a more accurate formulation, one's friendly rivals.

Such a framing ignores the ways that the trolling discourses of gamer culture affect women. Virtual archival projects like *Fat, Ugly, or Slutty* (by gtz) and *Not in the Kitchen Anymore* (by Jenny Haniver) catalog deliberate attempts to harass and target female gamers who reveal their gender identities online (Figures 1–3). As the following examples (selected from among hundreds) show, a wide variety of policing strategies are deployed in performances of compulsive heterosexuality within gaming culture, including overt sexual objectification of women, slut shaming, body policing, and discourses of rape and domestic violence.[3] (I discuss this in more detail in Chapter 2.) Furthermore, many critics and gaming journalists ("R-Word" 2012; Hernandez 2012b; Thorn and Dibbell 2012) have written about "the tendency of 'rape' to be used by gamers as slang for victory over an obstacle or fellow player" (Salter and Blodgett 2012, 406), as in a winning combatant celebrating their success by screaming "you just got raped!" into the microphone attached to his headset.

Rape is even occasionally mentioned in professional promotional campaigns for games. For example, at the E3 games conference in 2013, Microsoft, maker of Xbox video game consoles, unveiled a new installment in the long-running fighting game franchise *Killer Instinct* (Double Helix Games, Microsoft Studios, 2013). During the demo, Torin Rettig, a male producer on the game, played a match against Ashton Williams, a female community manager from Microsoft, and the trash talk that Rettig engaged in to

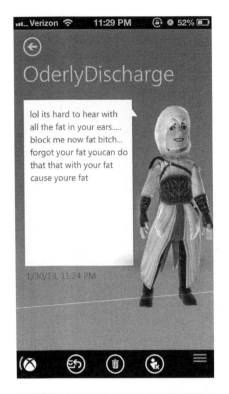

Figures 1–3. Body shaming, rape threats, and gendered insults: "Multitasking Fail," September 8, 2011; "Divine Calling," June 13, 2012; and "Sorry, What Are You Trying to Say?," February 18, 2013. Courtesy of gtz from *Fat, Ugly, or Slutty.*

spice up their fight for the audience devolved into a rape joke: "Just let it happen, it will be over soon," he told Williams. The crowd chuckled in response (gamespot 2013).

Microsoft later apologized for the "off the cuff and inappropriate comment" (Greenfield 2013) that was meant to be "friendly gameplay banter" and not "bullying and harassment of any kind" (Ngak 2013). However, the fact that a phrase so commonly associated with rape might be thought of by industry professionals as "friendly banter," that a presenter at "gaming's biggest trade show in North America" (Takahashi 2016) would see no problem with directing such a phrase toward a female opponent, and that many in the audience would consider this the laugh line of the presentation point to the normalization of rape discourse in gaming culture.

This uncomfortable on-stage representation of gendered power dynamics strongly resembled those captured during the online reality show *Cross Assault* (Goldfarb 2012), a program about professional fighting game players sponsored by Capcom, the creators of classic fighting games like *Street Fighter* and *Darkstalkers* (Capcom, 1994), and the gaming news site *IGN*.[4] The show, which followed two teams of gamers as they competed for a $25,000 prize, was conceived as an elaborate advertisement for a new game: *Street Fighter X Tekken* (Capcom, 2012). But on the first day of broadcasting, the show featured competitors on Team Tekken sexually harassing their teammate, Miranda Pakozdi, during a practice session.

Pakozdi was continually pressured to present herself as a source of objectified gratification for the presumed straight male viewers of the live-streaming video feed. For example, her teammates suggested that she should challenge another female competitor to a mud wrestling contest, and she was pestered to reveal her bra size for the entertainment of the audience. Her team's coach and the instigator of the majority of these exchanges, fellow competitive gamer Aris Bakhtanians, even jokingly referred to the broadcast as "the harassment stream" (crossassaultharass 2012).

At first Pakozdi's reaction is to (somewhat nervously) laugh off these comments, but as the harassment continues, she gets more and more irritated. Her responses grow short and terse, and she begins to push back against her coach's lewd suggestions, which he insists he is making on behalf of the male viewers of the stream, as in this exchange:

BAKHTANIANS: Play for her thighs [as the prize for winning the match].
PAKOZDI: No.

BAKHTANIANS: Play for shirts. Loser takes their shirt off.

PAKOZDI: Hell no.

BAKHTANIANS: Look, I'm the coach here, Miranda. I don't wanna hear anything out of you.

PAKOZDI: Okay, no. I'm trying to play, Aris! You're messing me up.

BAKHTANIANS: You need to be able to focus when people are heckling you!

PAKOZDI: That's fine! But, like, this is just creepy.

BAKHTANIANS: You need to be able to play when people are harassing you.

PAKOZDI: Thanks for that, Aris . . .

BAKHTANIANS: Take off your shirt. . . .

BAKHTANIANS (to the viewers of the stream): I tried asking if she has a skirt so we can hook you guys [in the chat] up tomorrow, but she didn't bring a skirt.

PAKOZDI: Nope.

BAKHTANIANS (to Pakozdi): Maybe we'll go to the store and get you a skirt.

PAKOZDI: I'm good.

BAKHTANIANS: I'm serious! Can I go to the store and get you a skirt? I'll pay for it. . . . (To viewers) Do you see what I do for you guys, chat? I'm gonna try and get her a skirt, guys. I got your back. Out of my own pocket, I'm gonna buy her a skirt. If I can't buy her a skirt, I'll make her a skirt out of napkins. (To Pakozdi): You're wearing a skirt. Miranda, you're wearing a skirt tomorrow.

PAKOZDI: I don't have a skirt.

BAKHTANIANS: I'm gonna buy you one. (crossassaultharass 2012)

Bakhtanians enlists the broader fighting gaming community to pressure Pakozdi into tolerating his behavior. He implies that by taking offense to his statements, she is failing to conform to the expectations of the community in multiple ways. First, she risks failing at the competitive level because her supposedly overly emotional responses to his taunts distract her from her game. A better competitor, he implies, would be able to rise above the taunts and ignore them to concentrate on the game. By exhibiting an emotional response, Pakozdi marks herself as an inadequate teammate. Second, he uses the audience watching the stream as a weapon to pressure Pakozdi into indulging him. He implies that her protests about sexual harassment are akin to disloyalty to her team and to the broader fighting game community watching the show. Bakhtanians constantly invokes "the chat"—the viewers watching the show as it streams live and commenting on the action in a chat room attached to the stream. He encourages the chat room participants to join in as he pesters Pakozdi and narrates back to her their contributions: "This chat is, like, evolving. There's already people who have names registered as parts of your body. . . . They're getting grimier and scummier" (crossassaultharass 2012). "Are you a part of this team, Miranda?" he finally asks, a question that might apply to the competitive team, or to the team of the fighting game subculture (crossassaultharass 2012). If the answer is yes, he implies/threatens, then she should refrain from pushing back against his antics and acquiesce to his (and, according to his construction, the fans') desires by tolerating the harassing language.

A few days after the broadcast, Bakhtanians rationalizes the harassment in a conversation with Jared Rea, the community manager of *Twitch.tv*. In this exchange, Bakhtanians responds with indignation to the idea that the fighting game community should work to become more inclusive toward female players and spectators. He declares that sexual harassment and fighting games are "one and the same thing" (iplaywinner 2012): "The sexual harassment is part of a culture. And if you remove that from the fighting game community, it's not the fighting game community." "These things are established for years" he told Rea, adding, "It's not right . . . it's ethically wrong" for the community to be asked to change its trolling behavior to court a bigger, more diverse group of potential participants.

> And I know you think that, oh, what do you know about ethics? All you do is say racial stuff and sexist stuff. But, you know, those are jokes, and if you were really a member of the fighting game community you would know that. You would know that these are jokes. . . .
>
> The beauty of the fighting game community, and you should know this—it's based around not being welcome. That's the beauty of it. That's the key essence of it. (iplaywinner 2012)

Bakhtanians thus posits trash talking, and sexual and racial harassment in particular, as a kind of hazing that competitive gamers must pass through in order to earn a spot in the community.[5]

Google Bombs, Beat-Em-Ups, and Dickwolves

TROLLING AS AN MMORPG

In addition to policing their own spaces, trolls also sometimes venture into other online communities to target those whom they perceive as a threat (or at the very least a nuisance) to their culture. There have been several high-profile instances of trolling aimed at feminists who criticize the gaming community. One of them was the *Penny Arcade* Dickwolves incident, in which a well-known, long-running web comic dedicated to gaming culture ran a strip that featured the rape of a (male) slave by a lycanthrope as a setup to its punch line. The strip was intended as a jab at the sometimes amusingly callous questing systems featured in MMORPGs like *World of Warcraft*, which often require heroes to help a specific number of citizens to receive a reward, then cut off the quest even though the player can plainly see that more people in need of help remain for other heroes to encounter. The comic opens with an enslaved nonplayer character (NPC) begging a hero for help and describing the details of his hellish existence, including the fact that he and his fellow slaves get "raped to sleep by the dickwolves" each night. Unfortunately for the poor NPC, the hero/player has already fulfilled his quota for this quest and responds, "I only needed to save *five* slaves. Alright? Quest Complete" (Holkins and Krahulik 2010c). Soon after the strip's publication, some feminist commentators on blogs like *Shakesville* (Millie A 2010) criticized the comic for choosing rape as the topic of the quest, arguing that the same fundamental joke about *World of Warcraft*'s quest mechanics could have been made about any number of less triggering topics.

The controversy might have ended right there, with one website making a comic strip with the intention of making gamers laugh and readers on another website declaring that they found the joke to be in poor taste. However, instead, *Penny Arcade* creators Jerry Holkins and Mike Krahulik (known more commonly by their pen names, Tycho and Gabe) and their fans reacted to the criticism with a multipronged trolling strategy designed to further fan the flames. First the duo published a second comic mocking the supposed concerns of (straw) feminist commentators. This strip is framed as a sit-down with the creators, in which Tycho scolds any hypothetical readers who might have decided to become rapists as a result of reading the comic. Gabe declares, "We want to state in clear language, without ambiguity or room for interpretation: we hate rapers, and all the rapes they do. Seriously though. Rapists are really the *worst*" (Holkins and Krahulik 2010a).

Of course, this comic was designed to troll: it frames those who expressed concerns about the original Dickwolves joke as overly emotional, irrational, and illogical. In the blog post accompanying this second comic, Krahulik insinuates that these critics must come from a place "outside" of *Penny Arcade* fandom. He expresses doubt that anyone who follows the strip would actually be offended by the joke, implying that those who *did* take offense were Johnny-come-latelies whose unfounded opinions could safely be ignored by true fans:

> What surprised me most about some of the reactions to our Dickwolf joke was not that people were offended. But that this was the comic that offended them. In each case the emails I got started with something like "I've been a long time fan" or "Been reading the comic for years . . ." and then they go into how this particular comic really bothered them.
>
> I just don't understand that. Did the comics about bestiality, suicide, murder, pedophilia, and torture not bother them? . . . What comic strip have they been reading all these years? (Krahulik 2010)

The implication behind this line of argument is that critics of the strip had not actually been reading for years, that they were actually new readers (or perhaps first-time visitors who had read about the comic on a feminist blog), that they were outsiders to the *Penny Arcade* community and therefore ideal targets for the game of trolling.

Some *Penny Arcade* readers joined the rhetorical battle by flooding feminist online spaces and violating their posted rules of conduct (led by Krahulik himself in one instance; see McEwan 2010) and by tweeting rape threats and death threats (Stanton 2011a). This pile-on can be read as an attempt by *Penny Arcade* fans to demonstrate to both Holkins and Krahulik (who function as "power brokers" [Salter and Blodgett 2012, 404] or celebrities in the video game community) and to each other that they are hardcore fans. They demonstrate their allegiance to *Penny Arcade*—and by extension to the broader gaming culture that *Penny Arcade* represents—by exhibiting a devil-may-care attitude themselves while disrupting the peace of their virtual enemies, generating reactions of anger, violation, disgust, and even fear.

At one point the *Penny Arcade* store even began selling Dickwolf T-shirts to its fans so they could publicly show their support for the duo's epic troll at the 2011 Penny Arcade Expo (PAX for short). Ironically, PAX is a video game convention that markets itself as a safe and inclusive space for all ("Safety and Security" 2013). Anastasia Salter and Bridget Blodgett note that "the spots-team design" of these T-shirts "seemed to offer an implicit team-spirit endorsement of rape as a joke" (2012, 407) and encouraged "wearers . . . to view others wearing it as allies" (408). Indeed, Courtney Stanton (2011b), one of the trolls' targets, described the shirt as a means of intimidation:

> I have to wonder at the creative meeting that spawned the final design—in my mind, it was a 10-second event that consisted of, "maybe we should have the word 'Dickwolves' on it somehow—" and then the fire alarm went off and they had to evacuate the building, never to continue the discussion. Given the hostile attitude Gabe and Tycho have continued to display toward the issue, I can't help but feel like they just want anyone who spoke out to walk into PAX East and be confronted with a wall of "Dickwolves" text at the official merch table. . . .
>
> The shirt design is a sports team style design using the word "Dickwolves" where the name of the team would usually go and with a little wolf-head logo, as if it was a team mascot (see also: every other sports shirt ever). Is there *any way* to read this shirt *other* than, "Go Team Rapists"?

The shirts were yet another troll, albeit one colocated in both the digital world and the physical one.[6] It would function as a test of all PAX attendees. Those who were offended by their presence would, in the eyes of the wearer, be outing themselves as someone who didn't get the joke in the original comic and, by extension, someone who doesn't get *Penny Arcade* fandom and gaming culture in general.

Another high-profile incident began when trolls targeted feminist commentator Anita Sarkeesian of the website *Feminist Frequency*. When Sarkeesian solicited funds via *Kickstarter* (a platform for funding independent projects where creators ask for money from backers, who receive rewards for pledging increasing amounts toward a project's budget) for a series of videos criticizing the portrayal of women in video games (Sarkeesian 2012e), she found herself targeted by trolls long before she was even able to release her first video. For example, she faced a barrage of negative comments on the *YouTube* video announcing the *Kickstarter* campaign including "many variations on common sexist troll posts like 'get back in the kitchen' 'tits or get the fuck out' and the old standbys 'slut,' 'whore,' and 'cunt'" (Sarkeesian 2012b). She also received a flood of pornographic images, including drawings of her being raped by video game characters (Sarkeesian 2012d). Her Wikipedia page was vandalized as trolls "chang[ed] the text, chang[ed] the page categories, chang[ed] the external links to re-reroute to porn sites and add[ed] a drawing of a woman with a man's penis in her mouth captioned with 'Daily Activities'" (Sarkeesian 2012c). She was also Google bombed[7] so that "her top Google search result return[ed] the sentence 'Anita Sarkeesian is a feminist video blogger and cunt'" (Plunkett 2012). She endured DDoS attacks[8] on her website, and hackers attempted to gain access to her e-mail and social media accounts (Sarkeesian 2012d). Hate sites targeting Sarkeesian even posted her home phone number and address in an attempt to intimidate her (Lewis 2012b).

Sarkeesian's case is strongly reminiscent of that of another prominent woman who faced an army of gamer trolls: Kathy Sierra. Sierra was once

> a well-known programmer and game developer [who] maintained a popular blog on software development called "Creating Passionate Users." In 2007, anonymous individuals attacked Ms. Sierra on her blog and two other websites. Posters suggested she deserved to have her throat slit, be suffocated, sexually violated, and hanged. They posted her home address and Social Security number. They posted doctored photographs of Ms. Sierra: one picture featured her with a noose beside her neck; another depicted her screaming while being suffocated by lingerie. After the attacks, Ms. Sierra canceled speaking engagements and feared leaving her home. (Citron 2009, 380–81)

But the most disturbing example of trolling Sarkeesian faced was the creation of a game in which players could *Beat Up Anita Sarkeesian* (Figure 4):

> On July 5th 2012 an interactive domestic abuse style "game" . . . was uploaded to the NewGrounds website by one of the site's users. It invited players to "punch this bitch in the face" and with each click a photoshopped image of me would become progressively more bloody and battered until the screen turned completely red. The "game" was

Figure 4. Screenshots from *Beat Up Anita Sarkeesian*. Courtesy of *Feminist Frequency*.

then proudly circulated on various gaming forums by those engaging in the sustained harassment campaign against me. It remained on New-Grounds website for about 24 hours before being removed. (Sarkeesian 2012d)

The game's description justifies its existence by an us-versus-them logic that pits gamers against feminists in a battle over self-expression and freedom of speech:

Anita Sarkeesian has not only scammed thousands of people out of over $160,000, but also uses the excuse that she is a woman to get away with whatever she damn well pleases. Any form of constructive criticism, even from fellow women, is either ignored or labeled to be sexist against her.

She claims to want gender equality in video games, but in reality, she just wants to use the fact that she was born with a vagina to get free money and sympathy from everyone who crosses her path. (Lewis 2012b)

By using the format of a game to contain this violent revenge fantasy, the troll attempts to ride the line between provocation and playfulness. The images used in the game are horrific and revolting, yet they are described as a form of play: the final screen of the game tells users, "Thanks for playing!" and invites them to "Play Again." By rhetorically positioning this kind of harassment as a game, trolls gets to have their cake and eat it too: they can evoke the desired reactions of outrage and disgust from their targets via the over-the-top violent imagery while creating a veneer of plausible deniability that their commentary on Sarkeesian is not a real threat but rather just a game or joke. Anyone who has an emotional reaction to their game must therefore be a joyless stick-in-the-mud who doesn't get gaming culture.

In a TED talk about her experience, Sarkeesian (2012a) identifies the trolling mentality writ large as a kind of game. She says that finding herself targeted by the trolls of the gaming community was like finding herself suddenly cast in the role of "the villain of a massively online game":

> All of my social media sites were flooded with threats of rape, violence, sexual assault, death. And you'll notice that these threats and comments were all specifically targeting my gender. What's even more disturbing, if that's even possible, than this overt display of misogyny on a grand scale is that the perpetrators openly referred to this harassment campaign and their abuse as a game. . . .
>
> Now we don't usually think of online harassment as a social activity but we know from the strategies and tactics that they used, that they were not working alone, that they were actually loosely coordinating with one another. This social component is a powerful motivating factor that works to provide incentives for players to participate, or perpetrators rather, to participate and to actually escalate the attacks by earning the praise and approval of their peers. We can kind of think of this as an informal reward system where players earn "Internet points" for increasingly brazen and abusive attacks. Then they would document these attacks and they would bring them back to the message boards as evidence, to show off to each other—kind of like trophies or achievements.

Even the attempts at hacking and vandalism she faced could be thought of as gamelike in nature. According to Orly Turgeman-Goldschmidt (2005), hackers often pose their hobby as a game that they play against the security systems of their victims, as opposed to a violation of their victims' personal privacy, and A. E. Adam (2003) notes that hackers sometimes describe their activities as pranks. Moreover, hackers exhibit gamelike behavior by competing with one another to top each others' exploits and establish hierarchies within their communities (Burrill 2008, 116–31). The true audience for their performances of technical virtuosity is not the victims of their hacking; it is the community of hackers to which they belong, just as the true audience for the troll is not the target but other trolls.[9]

Conclusion

Whether they are trolling for newbies within their own communities or infiltrating another virtual space, trolls see their actions as moves in a grand game—or, in the case of the video game subculture, a metagame that takes place inside of and around the electronic games that they play. Trolls imagine themselves as trickster figures and adopt a persona that is rude and obnoxious (or perhaps simply ignorant) to entertain themselves and their friends by infuriating others. Through this persona, they can expose their victims as humorless bores and "make them . . . look even more clueless than they already do, while subtly conveying to the more savvy and experienced that [they are] in fact a deliberate troll" (Wang 1998). As one troll wrote in an anonymous "Troller's FAQ," "The people who are going to get the maximum enjoyment out of your post are other trollers. . . . It is trollers that you are trying to entertain so be creative—trollers don't just want a laugh from you they want to see good trolls so that they can also learn how to improve their own in the never ending search for the perfect troll" (Wang 1998). The victims of trolling are simply game tokens being exchanged by the trolls in their effort to prove their mastery over this rhetorical game of "identity and deception" (Donath 1998, 45).

I read the use of trolling as a mechanism to police online communities (and particularly the online gaming subculture) as a highly gendered act. The rules of the game of trolls, in addition to the content of messages commonly used to troll, enforce a set of community standards that value the performance of traits traditionally considered masculine like objectivity, calm self-possession, and emotional distance and that devalue traits that have been typically imagined as feminine, such as emotional engagement and earnestness. After all, the primary way that trolls distinguish themselves from their victims is through the manipulation of emotions. Trolls win when they are able to elicit an emotional response from their victims while maintaining a cool, level-headed image for themselves. This is true regardless of the content of their hurtful messages. Many trolls do choose to use gendered insults to provoke their victims. But even in cases where their barbs are gender neutral, the trolls' aim is to trick victims into temporarily losing their ability to adequately enact a textual performance of masculinity. Gender is the conceptual field upon which the game of trolls is played.

This was made abundantly clear as #GamerGate captured the attention of the mainstream media (see Chapter 4). #GamerGate is important because it was exceptionally well organized—but it is not unprecedented. It is merely an especially intense version of the same kinds of trolling games that have been a part of online gaming culture for decades.

Yet it is perhaps not the trolls themselves who do the most to curtail female participation in gaming culture. Rather it is the widespread acceptance of trolling by the Internet at large that acts as the most effective deterrent. Trolling, particularly trolling aimed at women, is generally thought to be an inevitable part of life on the Internet, a risk that women knowingly take when they go online. Danielle Keats Citron argues that "the public and law enforcement routinely marginalize women's experiences [of trolling], deeming the harassment harmless teasing that women should expect, and tolerate, given the Internet's Wild West norms of behavior" (2009, 373). Citron notes that trolling victims are dismissed as "overly sensitive complainers" (375) and "drama queens" (396) who "assumed the risks" associated with presenting as female on the Internet and thus should have known that trolls would be coming their way (375).[10] One might characterize this aloof attitude as itself a massively multiplayer act of trolling perpetrated by the community as a whole. The message being sent by this wholesale dismissal of women's experiences of harassment in the gaming community is, to use the trolls' parlance: "If you are too butthurt to hang with us, then you should leave."

But trolling is not inevitable. In fact, it is seen as an undesirable feature of the community by many game producers, who are working to implement features that will curtail trolling in an attempt to broaden their player bases and make their games more welcoming to new players (see Chapter 3). For example, the world's most popular multiplayer online battle arena game, *League of Legends*, formerly implemented a Tribunal punishment system for players who are regularly reported to be trolls. And Microsoft's Xbox One console boasts "advanced troll detection" software designed to weed trolls out of the general multiplayer population and pair them up to play with each other (Scullion 2013).

However, while game makers have a monetary incentive to curtail trolling behavior, regular gamers actually experience an incentive to pretend that trolling is an ingrained and unavoidable part of the gaming community, and therefore that female gamers are the ones to blame if they are upset by a barrage of harassers online. Such a cynical attitude toward trolling marks one as an urbane, experienced cultural insider who is immune to the emotional damage that the trolls are trying to create.

It is tempting to imagine the geeky world of online gaming as an equal-opportunity environment, one where women and men exist on an equal playing field. We want to believe that on the Internet, where physical bodies are unimportant in comparison to textual and technical performances, anyone can rise to the top of the social hierarchy, regardless of gender. However, participants are only able to do so when they use the anonymity provided by the Internet to construct a persona in keeping with the new (male) geek chic. Girls can play alongside the boys, but only insofar as they can make themselves seem to be like one of the boys. Queer people are welcome only so long as they work to avoid being seen as fags (see Chapter 3). Ironically, it requires a great deal of labor from both male and female participants in gaming culture to maintain a posture of effortless self-possession. Trolling is a game of aloofness and uncaring that actually requires a great deal of commitment to play.

In the next two chapters, I will discuss the special obstacles encountered by gamers who refuse the specific brand of coolness exemplified by the troll and explore how gamer culture works to explain and contain the ruptures in the social order posed by their refusal to conform to the hierarchy of geeky masculinity. In Chapter 2, I argue that the encroaching perception that gaming culture will be feminized by the influx of women and girls into geeky cultural spaces threatens those who define their self-worth according to the game of masculinity described above. I use examples from the recent explosion of visual and verbal memes about female gamers flourishing online to explain how these new entrants into gamer culture are reimagined as figures that are less threatening to the status quo. These memes revolve around three stereotypes that circulate about female gamers: that they only play games because they were introduced to them by their straight male partners, that they are mostly casual gamers with poor taste and poor gaming skills, and that they are mere pretenders who only seem to be into gaming because they want to trick gamer guys into giving them money and attention that they do not deserve. Such narratives represent an attempt to ignore what Judith Butler (2007) has famously called "gender trouble," a troubling posed by women who play games by recasting them as traditional feminine archetypes like the subservient, sexy sidekick, the incompetent, childlike dilettante, and the unscrupulous whore. In Chapter 3, the ghost of the faggot will rise to haunt us as queer gamers and their allies take to the Internet and lobby for the inclusion of gay and lesbian relationships in online role-playing games.

Game Break

Far Cry 3

THE HEART OF DARKNESS

n *Far Cry 3* (Ubisoft, 2012), you can hang glide into battle and drop down onto your foes like some kind of tropical Batman. You can set a tiger loose in an enemy base and watch the chaos from afar, or you can sneak up on each of the guards and slit their throats, one by one. You can use a flamethrower to burn down an entire marijuana field, and experience trippy visuals and music as your avatar gets high from the smoke. You can do just about anything a bro's heart desires. And, according to lead writer Jeffrey Yohalem, that is the point.

Yohalem describes *Far Cry 3* as a "meta-commentary of videogames. So it's talking about not just shooters, but videogames as a whole, and what we've turned a blind eye to in videogames" (Lejack 2012). Yohalem explains,

Videogames have all these tropes that they use again and again because they're easy to design for. I tried to do something where we take those tropes and we subvert them so that they become revealed. We're revealing what's weird about these tropes, and also we're trying to explore them from a fresh perspective. . . .

> For instance there's a torture scene in *Far Cry 3* that is trying to
> call to attention how strange and unsettling torture scenes in video-
> games are. The context of that torture scene in *Far Cry* is meant to
> really shock the player in a way that other torture scenes in games try
> to make the player feel comfortable with torture. We're trying to do
> the opposite. The use of sex and violence in the game is similarly call-
> ing attention to appropriate and inappropriate uses of those things.
> (Lejack 2012)

The game is essentially a composite of the colonialist fantasies that are
common to the medium. You play as Jason Brody, a millennial adrift in his
own life who decides to go find himself on a tropical adventure vacation.
When he and his group of friends accidentally skydive onto Rook Island,
however, they realize they bit off a lot more than they could chew. They
are kidnapped and held for ransom by the nefarious Vaas Montenegro, the
right-hand man of the island's resident kingpin, Hoyt Volkner. Jason barely
escapes. He is taken in by the island's native tribe, the Rakyat, who are in
awe of the fact that he got away from Vass alive, and their leader, Citra Ta-
lugami, who attempts to convince him that he is the ultimate warrior fore-
told by their prophecies, and who guides him through the tribe's sacred
rituals so he can rescue his friends.

   If that sounds like a typical story of a white male savior exploring a savage land and rescuing a primitive people, it is supposed to. Yohalem compares the game's setting to "Never-Neverland" (Lejack 2012), and Joseph
Bernstein (n.d.) describes Jason's journey as "Kurtzian," referencing Joseph
Conrad's classic colonialist novel *Heart of Darkness* (1899).[1] *Far Cry 3* holds
up a mirror to the racist and sexist fantasies that drive our escapist enter-
tainments and is designed, according to its creator, to make us reflect with
discomfort on the kinds of real human pain we are happy to use as a backdrop for our fun. For example, he describes how the game's many distract-
ing opportunities for mayhem seemingly contradict Jason's overarching
goal to rescue his friends:

> I love when people online talk about, "Oh I don't understand, the game
> tells me I'm saving Jason's friends, but then I'm going off and doing all
> the open world stuff and I'm not doing any story missions." But *that's*
> the story of the game. Players are choosing that to such a degree that
> they think this is all an accident. But it's not! . . .

> A lot of games are talking about killing as human, which is differ-
> ent than killing in videogames. Is killing a good thing in the real world?
> That's not the question this game is asking at all. It's not an examina-
> tion of human beings as killers in reality. It's an examination of what
> you feel when you play a videogame. And I think that question is fresh
> still, and worth examining. (Lejack 2012)

As Jason comes to enjoy his time on the island, and as his friends become
more and more terrified of his willingness to indulge in his darker side,
players are asked to consider the violence threaded through their entertainment.

The game attempts to grapple with the dehumanizing of women and
people of color that occurs as an integral part of these fantasies. It is rife
with references to rape and sexual assault. As I described in Chapter 1,
gaming culture often uses the rhetoric of rape as shorthand for in-game
dominance. *Far Cry 3* makes this power dynamic an explicit part of its narrative, turning rape into a real threat faced by Jason and his friends. At the
start of the game, when Jason's group has first been captured, Vass taunts
them and questions their manhood, saying things like "I am the one with
the dick" and "You're my bitch."

Shortly after Jason breaks free, he meets Dennis Rogers, Citra's second in command, who attempts to entice Jason into working to help the
Rakyat by promising him the tribe's women as a reward, thereby giving him
a chance to reclaim his masculinity. Indeed, as players explore the island,
they witness Volker's men abusing native women who have been captured
and forced into prostitution. At one point a male friend is sold into slavery
and, it is strongly implied, raped by his captor, who also forces the player to
call him "sir" (Hernandez 2012a). Even the game's leveling mechanic has a
metaphorical undertone of rape. Players augment their combat abilities by
getting sacred tattoos.[2] The island's culture literally gets under Jason's skin,
penetrating him. His first marking is administered by Rogers while he is unconscious, without his prior knowledge or his consent.

At the end of the game, Jason is offered a choice to either murder his
girlfriend, Liza Snow (uncoincidentally named after something pure and
white), and claim his place at Citra's side, or to save her and leave the island
behind. The latter is the "good" ending and thus is likely to be considered
the real ending or the one you are supposed to get. It concludes with Jason
returning home and declaring (despite turning into a violent murderer on

the island), "I am still, somewhere inside me, more than that, better than that." But if you choose to side with Citra, you get the "bad" ending, which, according to Yohalem, is the ultimate inversion of video games' typical treatment of sexism, rape, and sexual violence. If you choose to join Citra, you kill your girlfriend and your friends in order to earn your final tattoo and be inducted into the ranks of the Rakyat warriors. While under the influence of ceremonial hallucinogens, Citra conceives a child with Jason (that is, she drugs and rapes him), then murders Jason as a form of human sacrifice. According to Yohalem,

> Jason conjures up this whole idea that Citra needs saving and he's gonna save her, when in reality it was all a ritual she created to find a sperm donor, and she kills him. . . .
>
> Sex, violence, and the player is killed. Here are the things that satisfy our animal side as men, but they're subverted because it's a female doing it. . . . Now that I'm thinking about it, that final scene should have been Citra castrating Jason. Seriously, that's the point! It is like, "You win, motherf*****!" It's totally like, "F*** you, you misogynist idiot!" (Matulef 2012)

This ending, the writer explained, would be akin to "Princess Peach stabbing Mario" at the end of *Super Mario Bros.* (Matulef 2012).

Many critics were unconvinced of the effectiveness of the intended satire, seeing the game's supposedly tongue-in-cheek racism and sexism as indistinguishable from de rigueur racism and sexism in first-person shooters.[3] For example, in an interview with Yohalem (who went on a public relations tour to defend the game the week after its release), John Walker (2012) asked,

> Do you not think that part of the problem . . . comes from the fact that the majority of games' stories are as bad as the thing you're parodying? They are atrocious. So people come into a game expecting these incredibly immature and incredibly simplistic, and often incredibly stereotyped storylines, so when they approach *Far Cry 3*, instead of saying "This is an arch commentary on that," they say, "Well this is another one of what most games are like."

Paul Tassi (2012) observed,

Yohalem and *Far Cry* are sort of victims of their own medium. We're so
used to games with over-exaggerated stories that we don't really stop
to read much into a plot like this. Games have taught us for a long time
to almost always take things at face value. In video game land, a white
guy killing pirates on an island to save natives didn't seem so ridiculous
compared to other past stories, and most of us didn't bother to examine if there was a larger point trying to be made.

Dave Their (2012) concurred, calling the game "a sort of violent tourism,"[4]
and Jim Sterling (2012a) said that the game "appears cynical, not satirical. As
he says, it's a fantasy we've seen in pop culture cinema, but it's recreated
so faithfully in *Far Cry 3*, it cannot be considered as exaggerated—it's just
another example of the trope." But *Far Cry 3* also misfires in that it fails to
correctly attribute the source of the tropes it claims to be satirizing. If the
game is supposed to be about the kinds of violent delights provided by the
video game industry, then it is strange for the game to locate Jason's violent
transformation on a tropical island populated by people of color. Sure, Jason
might have been aching for the chance to play "white messiah" (Walker
2012) because of what he has been taught by Hollywood and the video game
industry, and therefore he has been dreaming of the chance to visit a place
like Rook Island to test his mettle. But the fact remains that within the
world of the game, the island really is inhabited by animalistic, tattooed,
sex-crazed, superstitious, uncivilized natives. The game turns an image of
the savage that was created by white folks (an image designed to rational-
ize and justify colonialism) into a reality. This is not a reversal of colonialist
discourse; it is a repetition of it.

A truly unexpected subversion of the trope would not consist in Jason
encountering, being polluted by, and ultimately being destroyed by the
same violent, passionate indigenous forces that plagued Conrad's Kurtz.
Instead, imagine a game in which Jason discovers that instead of the tribal
savages he thought he was rescuing, Citra and her tribe were secretly CIA
agents or international spies using a complex cover story to fool and ultimately apprehend the drug kingpin hiding out on Rook Island. At the end of
the game, the big twist would be that Jason's meddling was actually en-
dangering their mission and that his own bigoted assumptions about what
kind of people he would find on the island were what put him and his friends
in jeopardy. He (and by extension the player) would return home ashamed of

his ignorance rather than triumphant, and his stereotype-laden ideas about third-world people would be upended rather than confirmed.

Furthermore, if we extend the metaphor at the heart of this individual game and apply it to gaming culture more generally (as Yohalem seems to be implying we should), the lesson seems to be that the Internet itself, like Rook Island, is a wild, untamed space that tempts us into behaving against our better judgment. In reality, as I argue throughout this book, violent, racist, and sexist behavior is something that we brought online with us. It is just another place where we have extended the toxic racist and sexist fantasies that we have deployed everywhere else. The Internet doesn't make us into assholes. We simply imported our usual brand of assholery onto the Internet.

Sexy Sidekicks, Filthy Casuals, and Fake Geek Girls

MEME-IFYING GENDER IN THE GAMING COMMUNITY

TROLLING IS ONE OF THE primary mechanisms through which a masculine style of identity performance is normalized in gamer culture. However, because this digital form of masculinity, like all forms of masculinity, is a posture—a set of presentational practices and not some innate essence that is only accessible to male bodies—it is an unreliable mechanism for distributing access to power and privilege exclusively to men. Both men and women can deploy masculine performances, especially in online spaces where those performances need not be anchored in a particular physical body. This fact fosters anxiety about the social order. The porous nature of the border marking off gaming as a male activity is acknowledged by the impulse to guard it even more fiercely. The demographic data show that this anxiety might be well founded. Women are making their way into gamer culture in ever-increasing numbers. According to the Entertainment Software Association, almost half of all people who report playing play digital games (45 percent) are female ("Game Player Data" 2013), and in the coveted twenty-four- to thirty-five-year-old demographic, women now outnumber men nearly two to one according to the Consumer Electronics Organization (Brightman 2006). Female gamers are crucial to the success of the top-selling game franchise of all time, *The Sims* (Maxis, Electronic Arts, 2000): 65 percent of the audience for that franchise are women and girls (Boyes 2007). Women were also an important factor in the previous round of the video game console wars between the Nintendo Wii, the PlayStation 3, and Microsoft's Xbox 360. According to Neilson pollsters, the Wii became the "best-selling of the three systems" not by pursuing the "hardcore gaming segment" ("Every Gaming System Has Its Fans" 2009) but by specifically targeting "women, families and all those not typically associated with 'serious' gaming" ("Case Study" 2013), thereby enabling Nintendo to claim a "9 million player advantage among female console gamers" (Totilo 2009).

These examples pose challenges to the gendered system that distributes the imprimatur of legitimacy and belonging within gamer culture. If women are breaking into, or have broken into, gaming, then what will happen to this social system that has shaped the gaming world since its infancy? The entry of these women and girls into gaming culture threatens the status quo. They are making "gender trouble" (Butler 2007, xi) within gamer culture—trouble for the gender system we rely on to describe and assign social roles to subjects within that culture.

In *The History of Sexuality*, Michel Foucault (1990) outlines one way that such systems flex and adapt to accommodate challenges: by encouraging an intensification and a proliferation of discussion around problematic subjects, rendering them knowable (and thus containable) within that system's parameters. Once outsiders or perceived abnormal individuals are named, explained, and labeled as a particular type of person with its own regular and predictable features, they can be reintegrated back into the existing system. This is the rhetorical tactic at work in video game culture around the problem of the female gamer. The questions that the existence of a new influx of female gamers poses to the gendered hierarchy of gamer culture produces a "will to knowledge" (12), a desire to explain and hence to contain female gamers, thereby making them legible within existing gendered paradigms. We see this happening in the "veritable discursive explosion" (17) around female gamers that has been taking place both in the gaming industry and in the community.

The product of all of this discussion about girl gamers is a set of overlapping and interlocking descriptions of the types of girls who game, a taxonomy of the species of gamer girls that one might encounter online. Much of the discourse around women in games functions to corral female gamers into one of these diagnostic categories. Fitting a woman into one of these types aligns her with one of the familiar, commonsense beliefs about femininity that is accepted within the larger system. Thus, it renders her knowable within that system even as her very presence registers as a point of resistance against it. In fact, her initial resistance and subsequent recuperation serve to reinforce the circuits of power that sustain it.

One of the primary vehicles for these discussions are Internet memes, those viral or "spreadable" (Jenkins, Ford, and Green 2013) nuggets of content that proliferate on message boards and in comment sections throughout the web. I have identified three types of women who have been invented by and are continually cited in popular memes within gaming culture. The first is the sexy sidekick, the fantasy of what a gamer girl supposedly should be like. She is the subject of many wishful thoughts and the romantic interest of many popular books and movies featuring straight male gamers as protagonists. She is put on a pedestal by the gaming community as the perfect romantic partner for a gamer guy, the standard against which all actual female gamers are measured and found wanting in some way. She is typically described as being into gaming only because she has a boyfriend who was into it first. She props up the masculinity of her partner, and she supports him in game (as a helper character class like a healer) and in real life (as a talisman that proves his virility and sexual accomplishments to his fellows). The second type is the casual girl gamer, the dabbler who is too inexperienced and ignorant about gamer culture to understand its depths. She might play some digital games, but she stays out of the ultramasculine spaces populated by hardcore gamers, so she can easily be dismissed as not being a true gamer. The third type is the fake nerd girl. She isn't actually into gaming but is practicing a deception to get something (money, time, attention) out of a gamer guy. She is a villainess, someone who is looking to use her feminine wiles to victimize others.

These diagnostic archetypes (which appear everywhere—fictional narratives about gamer culture, industry press releases, game advertisements, forum posts, and blog comment threads created by gamers themselves) are a means to police women and girls who participate in a traditionally masculine activity like gaming in order to reclassify them and to narrate their actions in such a way as to render them more comfortably recognizable as performers of classical feminine roles: the object of heterosexual desire; the inept, childlike dilettante; and the duplicitous whore. Internet memes are a prominent vehicle through which such stereotypes are exchanged and proliferated. Yet because of their ever-shifting, ever-evolving natures, even the most regressive memes can be taken up and redeployed toward new purposes. Female gamers are beginning to create countermemes decrying sexism in geek culture, thereby simultaneously cementing their nerd cred and pushing back against gendered hierarchies in online gaming.

Making (Gender) Trouble

SITES OF RESISTANCE AND THE WILL TO KNOWLEDGE

Butler defines "gender trouble" as those "non-normative . . . practices" that "call into question the stability of gender as a category of analysis" (2007, xi), making the rules of the game of gender visible and thereby revealing it as an institution of social power rather than a simple expression of some natural biological order. Gender trouble might involve taking existing signifiers of masculinity and femininity (including codes of dress and makeup, of body language and disposition, of activity and habit) and remixing them in unexpected ways—ways that call attention to gender as a thing we do and not a thing we are (xxii–xxiii). They have the potential to make spectators uneasy because they suggest it is possible to become unmoored within the gender system (xi) and therefore one's place in the social institutions organized around gender.

Foucault would describe "gender trouble" as an example of resistance, a force capable of "producing cleavages in a society . . . fracturing unities and effecting regroupings, furrowing across individuals themselves, cutting them up and remolding them" (1990, 96). According to Foucault's model, power and resistance are not the opposite of one another. They are constitutive of one another. Power perpetuates itself by responding to the challenges posed by resistance even as resistance redirects power into new channels, potentially opening up new spaces and alliances. This means that large-scale institutional shifts or changes in who can access power are less likely to be the product of a single revolutionary act and more likely to be the end result of a multitude of iterations of the cycle of interaction between power and resistance.

One of the most effective ways for power to interact with resistance is to study it. The pressures created by resistance foster a "will to knowledge" (Foucault 1990, 12) or a desire to speak, think, and write about a disobedient object of investigation. This is because as it is observed and defined, dissected and theorized, resistance is brought under the purview of existing authorities, institutions, and disciplines, which position it in relation to existing schemes of knowledge. That knowledge is then used to justify the ways power is deployed.

Within the system that both describes and constitutes gender, a system that extends into every aspect of our culture, gaming is understood to be a masculine institution. This allows for the production of certain kinds of gendered conversations within gaming culture even as it creates limits on which other types of conversations are legible, on how conversations are presented, and on who is authorized to speak. The current influx of female gamers into the culture constitutes resistance to that gender system in the form of gender trouble. Within the current system, these gamers are illegible. The threat they pose to the status quo generates a will to knowledge, a desire to develop new narratives to explain their presence in such a way as to preserve the overall system even as that system expands to accommodate their presence. New categories or roles are created for them to occupy that explain their presence, attributing it to what are thought of as traditionally feminine traits and drives. The anxiety created by the presence of these women is diffused as the questions they pose to the gender system are wrapped in protective layers of discourse.

On the Origin of Memes

THE EVOLUTION OF THE MIND VIRUS

The primary form of discourse I analyze in this chapter is the Internet meme. The term "meme" was first coined in 1976 by Richard Dawkins in *The Selfish Gene*. Dawkins described memes as a way of understanding the development of the intellectual lives of human beings according to evolutionary theory. Memes can be thought of as bits of culture that spread from mind to mind like viruses, reproducing and thriving (or disappearing and dying out) depending on how suited they are to the environmental niche created by the community or subculture in which it exists:

> Just as genes propagate themselves in the gene pool by leaping from body to body via sperms or eggs, so memes propagate themselves in the meme pool by leaping from brain to brain via a process which, in

the broad sense, can be called imitation. If a scientist hears, or reads about, a good idea, he passes it on to his colleagues and students. He mentions it in his articles and lectures. If the idea catches on, it can be said to propagate itself, spreading from brain to brain. . . . When you plant a fertile meme in my mind you literally parasitize my brain, turning it into a vehicle for the meme's propagation in just the way a virus may parasitize the genetic mechanism of a host cell. (2006, 192)

Examples of memes include "such things as popular tunes, catchphrases, clothing fashions, architectural styles, ways of doing things, icons, jingles, and the like" (Knobel and Lankshear 2007, 199), as well as more abstract notions like the idea of God or, as I will argue below, the idea of gender as a social category.

What about individual agency? Some, like Susan Blackmore (1999), argue that human minds are little more than passive carriers for memes, computers that are operated by their memetic software and not active shapers of the cultural ecology. I, on the other hand, agree with scholars like Jenkins, Ford, and Green (2013) and Limon Shifman (2014), who argue that people can and do (and indeed must) purposefully and creatively contribute to the process of meme selection, propagation, and proliferation. Communal and subcultural "social norms, perceptions, and preferences are crucial in memetic selection processes" (Shifman 2014, 12). Certain memes take off within a particular community because that community's members select them for sharing: "Audiences play an active role in 'spreading' content rather than serving as passive carriers of viral media: their choices, investments, agendas, and actions determine what gets valued" (Jenkins, Ford, and Green 2013, 21). These memes are more likely to be shared when they speak to or with the existing discourses and memes that were already present in a given community. According to Limon Shifman, "At any given moment, many memes are competing for the attention of hosts; however, only memes suited to their sociocultural environment spread successfully, while others become extinct. Dawkins also noted that certain groups of co-adaptive memes tend to be replicated together—strengthening each other in the process" (2014, 9).

The memes I describe in this chapter are one such group of coadaptive memes—or, as Hans-Cees Speel (1996) calls them, memeplexes, which hang together and attach themselves to gendered anxieties around community membership and authenticity in gamer culture. They function as a kind of "(post)modern folklore, in which shared norms and values are constructed through cultural artifacts" (Shifman 2014, 14). As such, these memes affect how women and girls are portrayed in games, how they are marketed to (or ignored by) game development companies, and how they are received in online gaming communities.

Know Your Meme

THE LINGUA FRANCA OF INTERNET CULTURE

In the language of Internet culture, the colloquial meaning of the word "meme" is different from Dawkins's original construction. Internet memes are easily reproducible and remixable pieces of "observable audiovisual content, such as YouTube videos and humorous images" (Shifman 2014, 13), hashtags, image macros, and the like. "An Internet meme is always a collection of texts. . . . A single video is not an Internet meme but part of a meme—one manifestation of a group of texts that together can be described as the meme" (56). For example, a single, widely shared Photoshopped image is not a meme all by itself. However, if many Internet users begin to Photoshop that same image in different ways, then the sum total of all such images, with their unique mix of imitativeness and creativity, is a meme. Memes function as a means for community members to simultaneously display their own unique cleverness and to signal their conformity to community norms and their sense of belonging to the broader group (30). Many Internet memes serve these twin purposes by presenting themselves as language games or inside jokes. Like the game of trolling (see Chapter 1), visual and verbal memetic games help to distinguish cultural insiders (those who can correctly decode a meme and respond in kind) from cultural outsiders (those who need help understanding memes, those who lack the technical proficiency or the access to create their own, or those who continue to use memes that are generally thought to be unfashionable or over).

The Gamer Girl of His Dreams

SEXY SIDEKICKS

The first constellation of gaming culture memes I have identified concerns an elaborate romantic fantasy, a dream of what the ideal gamer girl might look like from the perspective of a geeky guy. One function of this imaginary girl is to transform the arrival of a possible rival into a sexy sidekick, a love interest who props up the masculinity of her partner rather than threatening it through competition. She games only alongside her male partner, and she makes her boyfriend look good to his fellows without ever showing him up by being more hardcore than he is. The memetic telling and retelling of stories featuring sexy sidekicks reassures those who might be feeling threatened by the appearance of women in gamer culture. The sexy sidekick is a prize who is distributed among men according to their ability to master technology in general or games in particular (Rubin 2011, 1). In other words, the initial challenge that female gamers pose to the gendered social order in gamer culture is neutralized as the story told about these fantasy women moves them from a stereotypically masculine position (a challenger, a competitor, a fellow combatant) to a feminine one (an object of desire, a love interest, a helpmeet who supports and nurtures her partner in his masculine pursuits).

The tale of a sexy sidekick often resembles the story structure of a video game. A relationship with one of these girls is like a battle with a video game boss: her initial hostility must be overcome by the geeky protagonist (using his elite gamer skills) if her affections are to be won. One example is Angelina Jolie's character, Kate, in the 1995 film *Hackers*. Kate is the most skilled high school–age hacker and gamer in New York City until Dade, the film's protagonist, moves to town. Dade is simultaneously smitten by Kate, annoyed by her aloofness and aggressiveness (naturally, Kate is portrayed as a man-hating feminist following in the footsteps of her mother, who writes self-help books about the uselessness of men), and finds himself in constant competition with her. The pair start up a rivalry when Dade beats Kate's high score on an arcade game, and from then on they continually try to outprank and outhack one another. They make a bet to see who can carry out the best revenge scheme on a Secret Service agent who had arrested one of their hacker friends, and the stakes revolve entirely around performances of masculinity and femininity, dominance and subservience. If Kate wins, she wants Dade to "become [her] slave," doing "shit work" on her hacking projects (essentially turning him into her helpful support). Kate is not just trying to outhack Dade. She is trying to outman (unman?) him—and in front of his all-male group of hacker friends. However, if Dade wins, he demands that Kate go on a date with him, during which she must present herself as pleasant and feminine; he tells her "you have to smile" and "wear a dress." Kate, meanwhile, continually makes emasculating comments to Dade, like telling him that her laptop is "too much machine" for him to handle and sarcastically remarking, "I hope you don't screw like you type." She even turns around Dade's sartorial request, telling him that if she wins the bet, *he* will have to don the dress.

As the film progresses, however, Kate finds herself stymied by a competing hacker's program, which she needs Dade's help to crack. Once he has proven, once and for all, that he has the superior skill set, she quickly softens toward him and relinquishes her prideful attitude, even allowing Dade to tell a police officer that "she knows shit [all] about computers" and that "she's just [his] girlfriend" in an effort to protect her. Whereas it is easy to imagine the scornful Kate we saw at the outset of the film taking umbrage at this dismissive statement, by the end of the film, she is thanking Dade for his paternalistic help. The film concludes with Dade and Kate's first date. She wears a dress with hose and garters underneath, blue eye shadow, mascara, and lipstick. He wears a jacket and pants. The threat Kate posed to Dade's manhood as the best hacker in his social circle has passed now that Kate has been thoroughly domesticated. She is no longer a rival to Dade's position. Instead, she supports him in it by coupling with him, and this support is represented by her submission to his romantic affections and her adoption of a softer, more feminine self-presentation.

An even more extreme version of the sexy sidekick fantasy centers on women who have literally been built to act as self-sacrificing supports. These fantasies depict the idealized gamer girl as a game girl, a digital construction made inside a computer program (because, these texts typically assume, the sexy sidekick is far too rare a bird for one to hope to encounter in the real world). She is a reward for the superior technical skills possessed by her creator, a piece of virtual loot he can show off to make himself look good. Mastery over technology is the same as mastery over these women because these women are a product of technology. The game girl is always already submissive to her man because she was programmed to be that way.

Take, for example, John Hughes's 1985 film, *Weird Science*. In this film, Kelly LeBrock's Lisa is a computer program made flesh. Like a literal Game Genie[1] whose only desire is to please her two masters, Gary and Wyatt, she was custom built to teach a pair of geeky guys about sex and relationships (since they are too unpopular at school for real girls to pay them any attention). Lisa is like a practice dummy they can use to level up into the kind of men who can get girls; she is a cheat code they use to initiate themselves into manhood, sexually and socially. Part of what makes her so perfect for this purpose is that she has no desires of her own. She makes no demands of Gary and Wyatt other than that they find happiness for themselves, and because their happiness is her happiness, they are not made to feel guilty for using her as a tool to prop up their social standing. For example, they use her as arm candy to show off to the jocks who used to taunt them. Lisa seems to be not only okay with this but also to thrill at being displayed in such a manner. Her sexual knowledge, her calm competency, and her technomagic powers are all rendered safe and unthreatening, as she only uses them to Gary and Wyatt's benefit (though they may not realize it at the time). She represents the fantasy that geeky gamer guys might achieve mastery over women using the same skill set they use to master their computers—a fantasy so popular that it was able to sustain a television spin-off series, also called *Weird Science*, that lasted for five seasons, from 1994 to 1998.

The notion that the ideal girl gamer is more interested in romantic attachments than in games themselves has made its way out of the fictional realm and into a meme espoused throughout the gaming community. Take, for example, the so-called fact that girls prefer to play supportive sidekick roles in collaborative multiplayer games. A quick perusal through forums dedicated to gaming as well as game-specific boards for titles like *World of Warcraft*, the world's most popular MMORPG (Birnbaum 2013), and *League of Legends*, the "most played video game in the world" (Gaudiosi 2013), reveals that gamers have bought into this meme, as threads pop up constantly with titles like "Why do girls always play healer priests and paladins?" (Glockass 2013), "Why do girls play healers in most cases?" (Nebulae 2012), "Why are Resto Druids and Healing priests always girls?" (Atkins 2014), "Are most healers female?" (Paladinjoe 2012), "Why do girls always play support???" (SorionHex 2013), and "its [*sic*] so weird why do 99% of girls play support" (KingofAsia 2013).[2]

There are several widely believed answers to this (faulty) question. The first is that these women only play in the first place because they have a (male) partner who introduced them to gaming; "under this logic, the 'unnatural' phenomenon of women wanting to play video games for many hours a week occurs as a side effect of their male relations" (Yee 2008, 86). It is assumed that these women would rather play a support class, someone who is there to heal their warrior partner's wounds or to buff up his stats, than a combat-oriented class. This narrative helps defang the gender trouble posed by a girl who plays games by recasting her hobby as an act of nurturing—a traditionally feminine task.

While it is true that, according to the census data gathered by Nick Yee in *World of Warcraft*, more women play alongside their romantic partners than men do (2008, 86), it is not the case that they overwhelmingly choose healing and support roles (Yee 2005).[3] Rather, this stereotype about female players' preferences derives from the way that women are often portrayed in the games themselves. The trope of woman as support character is common in classic role-playing games like *Final Fantasy X* (Square, 2001), in which female characters are given default skill sets and statistics that strongly incentivize players to use them for healing and support purposes—that is, they are programmed to be better at supporting than they are at fighting, or at the very least, it takes much more work to transform them into a successful damage dealer than it does to make them into a skilled healer, which they are programmed to naturally blossom into if given no specific attention. Female characters are so often programmed into support roles that male players in *World of Warcraft* who choose to play support and healing roles tend to do so using female avatars because they see such behavior as conforming to "expected behaviors and attitudes associated with their avatar's appearance" (Yee et al. 2011, 773). Thus, even though male and female avatars are statistically and functionally equivalent in terms of their ability to heal or deal damage in *World of Warcraft*, male players are more likely to assign healing roles to female avatars because to them, doing so seems to be a more authentic way of performing their character's gender.

This phenomenon emphasizes the influence that memes have over behavior. Repeated visions of female characters performing in supportive roles across multiple fictional narrative contexts combine with the notion that supporting and nurturing dispositions are an integral part of femininity itself to create the belief that female gamers must be interested in choosing to play supportive roles. In reality, the opposite is true: the role being performed (healer, support class) influences which gender will be chosen by the player. The narrative of their play is mapped onto the existing narratives seen within games.

Games that Even Your Mom Will Love

GENDERING CASUAL GAMES

In addition to turning female gamers into second bananas to their roman-tic partners, the supposition that women prefer to play support roles is also linked to the second meme used to explain the steady increase of female participation in gaming culture: the rise in popularity of casual games and the assumption that girl gamers are predominantly unskilled, neophyte casual gamers. One female player of *World of Warcraft*, Ori (2009), de-scribed this notion in a blog post: "There are two things that bother me about [the stereotype that girls only play healing and support classes]: the first being that there's always the implication that girls suck at video games, so that means healers must be easy to play, and the other is that there's the idea that girls play video games to support their boyfriends, who do all the cool stuff while we stand back and top off their health." Ori's second point is an apt description of the sexy sidekick stereotype, but her first point rep-resents a second meme, which suggests that one of the reasons that female players are thought to prefer support roles is because they only play games casually and therefore lack the skill to play the (presumably) more difficult classes (though there is nothing to suggest that healing and support classes actually are any easier to play successfully than other classes).

According to Jespar Juul (2010), casual gamers are often stereotyped as unskilled newbies ("noobs" in the parlance of the video game world) who prefer short gaming sessions playing games with simple controls—think *Bejeweled* (PopCap Games, 2001) or *Diner Dash* (Gamelab, Play-First, 2004)—over prolonged, intense, difficult gaming experiences. This cliché of the casual gamer is the mirror image of the hardworking hard-core gamer, who delights in challenge and dedicates hours to refining his skills. And I do mean "his." The video game industry nearly always assumes that the hardcore gamer is male (Juul 2010, 26), even as casual games are thought of (disparagingly) as games for girls. To be fair, the demographic data gathered by the gaming industry does show that, for example, down-loadable casual games for the PC and for portable devices like smartphones or iPads have a predominantly (71 percent) female player base (Juul 2010, 80). However, these numbers can be better explained by looking at the history of the video game industry and the various assumptions that businesses have built into their marketing strategies than by the supposedly inherent tastes and abilities of women.

Girls and women play casual games because the gaming industry tells them that casual games are the ones that were created with them in mind, and the industry tends to build casual games with girls in mind because they assume that the only way to reach a female demographic is to introduce them to the medium for the first time via an easy-to-play, watered-down game. That is, casual games have been traditionally marketed as appropriate (socially and in terms of mechanical difficulty or playability) for girls and women, while hardcore games are marketed to boys and men. The choice of which game to play becomes part and parcel of one's performance of gender, just as, according to Michael A. Messner (2000), choosing a baby doll or a GI Joe is one way for children to demonstrate that they have learned and can perform their own gender identities through play.

We have thus been taught to think of casual games as games for girls. At the same time, games marketed specifically to girls, which are often called "pink games" because of their over-the-top frilly, feminine art and their showcasing of girly toy franchises (Mattel's Barbie or the Disney princesses) and traditionally feminine tasks (fashion designer, hair and makeup artist, interior decorator, babysitter, and the double whammy: *Cooking Mama* [Office Create, Taito Corporation, Majesco Entertainment, and 505 Games, 2006]), typically follow the easy-to-play casual games design model. Historically this link dates to the 1990s, when well-meaning game developers like Purple Moon, which hoped to increase female participation in gaming and computer culture by creating some of the first-ever games marketed specifically to girls, bought into much of the game industry's essentialist assumptions about girls' (lack of) computer skills. These companies absorbed the industry assumption that a typical girl would not like video games or have much knowledge about them. Thus, when they went about conducting market research into the types of games that the typical girl might enjoy, they ignored the opinions of girls who already did play video games (after all, if they played games and knew about computers, they must be atypical, abnormal girls) and gave great weight to the opinions of girls who had no previous experience with gaming. The results of these surveys were a set of "very traditional feminine stereotype[s]" (Shaw 2009, 233) about what girls wanted. The surveys suggested that a hypothetical girl gamer would want games that placed a strong emphasis on "social relations, romance, emotions, and role-playing" (233), and that she would prefer games that required a low level of technical knowledge. From these skewed sources were born a raft of unsuccessful games that were widely considered boring and insipid and that tended to further isolate girls from the rest of gamer culture by portraying their interests as inherently different from those of boys (Eisenberg 1998). Despite the best of intentions on the part of girl-centric game developers, the history of girls' games was shaped by and came to reinforce the stale cultural narrative that video games are a masculine pursuit by operating under the same essentialist assumptions (that girls are low-skilled amateur players) that prevented games companies from marketing to girls in the first place. Pink games have been stuck in easy mode ever since.

In the wake of the failure of companies like Purple Moon, developers of casual games like PopCap Games are among the few companies in the game industry willing to take a chance marketing their work directly to women, or to make games around existing products and franchises that women and girls already like. This is because, in an industry where AAA blockbuster-style games can cost as much as $100 million to make (Cook 2013), larger developers are loath to take a chance on a demographic that, in their minds, has not proven to be full of loyal consumers of hardcore video games. They prefer to cater to the adolescent male market. Conversely, casual games can be made cheaply, are quicker to develop, and are easier for publishers to distribute than hardcore games (Hyman 2007), so casual games developers are in a better position to take risks on demographic groups beyond the adolescent male hardcore market. Indeed, they have a strong financial incentive to pursue these alternative markets because then they do not have to compete directly against the bigger, wealthier AAA game studios (Loeb 2013).

This would not necessarily be a problem, except the casual/hardcore split is not a neutral one—on the contrary. Casual and hardcore gamers are seen as belonging to separate castes; casual gamers are perceived as lacking something that hardcore gamers have (Vanderhoef 2013). They may lack ability; they may lack the commitment that would enable them to transition into playing hardcore titles; or they may lack the good taste to discern the difference between quality games and crap. Casual games are thought to be inferior, watered-down substitutes for players who can't handle hardcore titles. They aren't thought of as real games, and the people who play them aren't thought of as real gamers. As if to emphasize this fact, message boards with hardcore gamer constituencies, like *4chan* and *The*

Escapist forums, are home to a meme referring to casual players as "filthy casuals" (amanda b 2013; Sterling 2012b).

Because casual games are seen as games for girls, much of the rhetoric in hardcore circles deriding casuals is in service of the gendered social order within the gaming community. The new influx of female gamers can be dismissed as unworthy of notice because it is assumed that most of these girls are casual players. Furthermore, this discourse allows for the behaviors of fellow gamers to be disciplined along gendered lines: casual players are girly and thus occupy a low place in a social hierarchy that values masculine performance. John Vanderhoef (2013) provides examples of this latter phenomenon in his study of how hardcore gamers in online message boards frame discussions about casual games: "In addition to marrying the feminine with the casual space, part of this positioning of the other happens through the labeling of casual games as other in sexual orientation. To these particular gamers, hardcore games not only represent the masculine, they represent the heteronormative ideal. A discourse exists in this community that links casual games with homosexuality." As Erica Kubik puts it, "the end result" of this disciplinary discourse is the creation of "a normative value to the masculine hardcore gamer, and devaluation for the feminine casual gamer" (2012, 136).

This slippage between the feminine and the casual (and the notion that neither has a place in the hardcore gaming community, the only group of gamers worthy of consideration within the culture) also permeates the discourse of the games industry. Take for example the use of the term "girlfriend mode" by the developers of first-person shooters like *Gears of War 2* (Epic Games, 2008) and *Borderlands 2* (Gearbox Software, 2012) to describe a game's ability to "adjust . . . difficulty on the fly" so that it can "appeal to the casual audience" (Kohler 2008), or as John Hemingway, the lead designer on *Borderlands 2* team put it, so that players can share the game with someone who "suck[s] at first-person shooters" (Rundle 2012; see also Griffiths 2012b). The assumption behind this rhetoric is the same as the one behind the sexy sidekick stereotype: gamers are men, and their nongamer girlfriends suck so hard that they need a special, super easy mode if they want to try out their boyfriends' toys. Conversely, everyone who wants or needs to partake in the easier mode of play is labeled as girly. Games like *Resident Evil* (Capcom, 1996), which assign different difficulty curves to characters of different genders, reinforce these types of assumptions. Of this game, in which players can choose between a male and a female player character at the beginning of the game, Derek A. Bur-rill writes, "The female officer does not possess the same constitution as the male, so the female officer is equipped with more powerful weapons than the male officer. This clearly indicates that the creators of the game pro-jected heteronormative ideals onto the narrative as well as onto the needs of the player and expected a clearly delineated choice between men playing the male and women playing the female" (2008, 50). I would put it slightly differently. Rather than assuming that men play as men and women play as women, I would argue that this hardwired gendered setup demonstrates an association of the masculine with the hardcore skilled player and the femi-nine with the unskilled casual player. By virtue of choosing one mode of play or the other, one reveals whether or not they have the figurative balls to be hardcore. Players of either sex might very well choose the feminine position and thus reveal themselves to be girly when it comes to gaming, even as players of either sex might distinguish themselves as capable of handling the masculine mantle. Despite the uncertainty about the bodies of the actual players, the valorization of masculinity as a category (and the dismissal of its opposite) remains consistent.

Casual game developers also use gendered rhetoric to describe their work by eliding "non-traditional gamers" with "the proverbial mother-figure or *Mom*" (Vanderhoef 2013). Casual game designer Dave Walls quipped that he defines casual games as follows: "If my mom can play it, it's a casual game." Jason Kapalka (2006) says that they give new games the "Mom Test": "If our own moms could figure out a game without our help, that was a good sign." Once again, the least skilled players are assumed to be the female players, even by the very designers who are supposedly in-vested in catering to them. A casual game is defined one that is so easy that even a mom can figure them out.

Mainstream media coverage of casual gaming has picked up on this rhetoric as well. In a *New York Times* article on the pervasiveness of sexual harassment in online gaming, Amy O'Leary (2012) notes, "Jessica Ham-mer, a longtime player of video games and a researcher at Columbia Uni-versity, said the percentage of women playing such games online ranges from 12 percent to close to half, depending on the game type. Industry statistics from the Entertainment Software Association say 47 percent of game players are women, but that number is frequently viewed as so all-encompassing as to be meaningless, bundling *Solitaire* alongside *Diablo III*." This statement minimizes the massive increase in participation by women in digital gaming by comparing a casual game, *Solitare* (Microsoft, 1990), to a hardcore online game, *Diablo III* (Blizzard Entertainment, 2012). The implication is that only those who play hardcore games really count as gamers, and there are few women in that category. Casual female gamers are dismissed as irrelevant to a discussion of the gaming community because they don't play the right kinds of games.

Even all-time best-selling franchises like *The Sims* are often not thought of as real video games because their audience skews female. Instead, playing *The Sims* is likened in the *New York Times* to playing with a digital "dollhouse" (Schiesel 2006), a reframing that makes sense of girls' desire to play by recasting the game as a traditionally girly kind of toy. This allows the popularity of the franchise to be recognized while simultaneously protecting the idea that real video games are hardcore titles marketed to men. Coverage like this takes gendered assumptions about gamers for granted and explains data that seemingly disprove those assumptions by discursively rerouting whole swaths of female gamers into more traditionally feminine roles.

What about the girls who play hardcore games, who identify as gamers, and who participate in the kinds of activities that appeal to hardcore fans, like discussing games on message boards and attending gaming conventions? The presence of women in these traditionally masculine spaces constitutes a greater threat to the way gender is understood within gaming culture than does a statistical shift in the number of people playing digital games of all kinds. Another meme has developed around these women, one that takes the notion that women can't be real gamers and extends it to its logical conclusion: that any woman who appears to be a hardcore gamer must actually be a fake.

Checking Her Geek Cred

FAKE GEEK GIRLS

To fully understand the fake geek girl (or fake nerd girl) meme, it is useful to look back and see how it compares to the other discursive categories I discussed above. The sexy sidekick, be she a fictional character in a book or a movie about gamers or an imaginary *World of Warcraft* player who was drafted into playing a healer by her boyfriend, props up the masculinity of a gamer guy. And the girl as casual gamer casts femininity as the inferior archetype against which the hardcore gamer's masculinity is measured. However, neither of these stereotypes can account for the droves of women who are now participating in gamer culture and playing games competitively. These girls fall under another kind of disciplinary discourse, one in which every aspect of their geeky credentials is brought under intense surveillance. The burden falls on them to prove that they are not fake geeks and that they are not merely pretending to be into gaming in order to manipulate and emasculate gamer guys. This narrative casts masculinity as the victim of a duplicitous and predatory (yet simultaneously ignorant, ineffectual, and easily defeated) brand of femininity.

Accusations of fake geekdom come in several different flavors. The first takes the form of a demand that anyone in an online environment who claims to be a woman in real life must prove herself to be a woman in fact: the geek must prove that she is not a fake girl. Nick Yee found that players who use female avatars in role-playing games online, regardless of their actual sex and gender identity in the real world, report facing constant interrogation from players trying to discern the sex of the body operating the computer (2008, 93–94; see also Lin 2008, 70–71). For example, a user who claims to be female will often be inundated with requests for pictures to serve as proof, often via the dismissive demand that they provide "tits or get the fuck out" (Lindell 2012). Yee also found that players who use male-presenting avatars do not have to face these questions about their real-world identities on nearly the same scale (Lin 2008, 70–71, 93–94).

It is true that lots of female avatars in online games are operated by men (though not all of those who play as female avatars actually make the claim to be women in real life as well). These men report many different reasons for choosing female personas online. Some simply want to look at something they find attractive while they play (MacCallum-Stewart 2008), a claim that bolsters their own performance of heterosexual masculinity by reducing the female body of the avatar to an object over which they can assert mastery and control (Kennedy 2002; Burrill 2008, 57). Some express a desire to use a feminine mask to try and extort positive attention, favors, and gifts from other male players (MacCallum-Stewart; Lin 2008, 70).

Mika Lehdonvirta et al. (2012) have a more charitable description of this phenomenon in the Japanese MMORPG *Uncharted Waters Online* (Koei, 2005). They note that men often feel unable to ask for help lest they be seen as inadequate. These men "overcome their inhibition for help seeking when using female avatars" (29). That is, adopting a different visual presentation online makes them feel more authorized to break out of traditional gendered performances in other ways as "the individual adjusts their own behavior to be consistent with the gender of their self-representation, independent of the perceptions of others" (40). Yet the fact that these players associate a performance of seeking help as feminine and a performance of competent independence as masculine speaks to the general perception within gaming culture that female players are either newbies or unskilled players.

This idea is the subject of a meme: 4chan's "Rules of the Internet" (2007). Rule 37 states, "There are no girls on the Internet . . . ever." A popular derivative of this meme states that the Internet is a place where both the "men are men" and the "women are men" (Lindell 2012). Although this supposed fact is typically stated in tongue in cheek—in fact, the digital divide in terms of gender has essentially been erased as of the year 2003, when "the percentages of women and men online were exactly fifty–fifty" (Nakamura 2008, 154)—it represents a memetic truth that is reassuring to gamers invested in masculinity as a measurement of social worthiness.

Additionally, this meme ignores those online masquerades that are being conducted in the opposite direction; some female gamers choose male avatars, make the claim that they are men in real life, and/or simply refuse to answer questions about their real-world genders because doing so allows these women to avoid "verbal harassment, flirtation, surveillance, and endless efforts to determine the player's real gender" (Lin 2008, 70). As Nick Yee explains, "Many female players have learned that it is dangerous to reveal your real-life gender in MMOs because they will be branded as incompetent and constantly propositioned. In other words, they must either accept the male-subject position silently, or risk constant discrimination and harassment if they reveal that they are female" (2008, 94). These kinds of masquerades are not the subject of popular memes within the gaming community because they do not serve the gendered narrative that the community espouses. When women disguise themselves as men online, they expose the ways that the culture of masculinity in gaming overestimates the benefits that women are thought to experience online and underestimates the negative experiences that presenting as a woman can bring as well as the amount of privilege that adheres to those who perform a masculine persona in the gaming world.

This brings us to the other flavor of fake geek girl accusations, which has been receiving an increasing amount of attention over the last few years, both on news sites frequented by geeks and gamers (Hamilton 2012; Polo

2012; Sterling 2012c; Holkins and Krahulik 2016b) and in the mainstream press, including CNN (Peacock 2012) and *Forbes* (Brown 2012; Griffiths 2012a). It takes the form of a disciplinary discourse aimed at girls who are thought to be using gaming as a way to perform a malicious, predatory kind of femininity. According to this meme, there is a plague of girls who perform geekiness as nothing more than an affectation. These girls, the theory goes, are trying to trick geeky guys into giving them their attention, affection, and sometimes even their money (in the case of professional gamers and streamers, who earn money from their viewers in the form of donations and ad revenue) by pretending to be into video games when they really aren't.[4] Because of the supposed threat posed by these fake geek girls, all women in geeky gaming spaces become subject to heightened scrutiny, thereby making those spaces less hospitable to women and girls.

This framing defangs the gender trouble posed by the gamer girl by positing that a sizable number of the new female entrants into gamer culture are motivated not by their own desire to play and compete but rather by a desire to be pleasing to men. If a girl's geekiness is about earning a man's favor, then her actions both reaffirm male ownership of the pastime and reinforce a broader gendered hierarchy wherein women derive their self-worth from what men think of them (Pascoe 2007, 104). It is important to note that "girls frequently collude . . . in boys' discourses and practices of compulsory heterosexuality" (105) and thus echo and reinforce disciplinary discourse like this in an effort to "'bargain with patriarchy' by submitting to sexist social institutions and practices to gain other forms of social power" (104–5). In this case, women like Tara Tiger Brown (2012) can use talk of "fake geek girls" to bolster their own geek cred by contrasting themselves against the "bad" girls and aligning themselves with put-upon guys, thereby setting themselves up as one of the good ones. Brown writes:

> Girls who genuinely like their hobby or interest and document what they are doing to help others, not garner attention, are true geeks. The ones who think about how to get attention and then work on a project in order to maximize their klout, are exhibitionists. . . . Don't pretend to love something because you think it will get you attention. Don't think that you can take a shortcut because there isn't one. Dig deep, dig to the roots, dig until you know things that others you admire in the subject matter don't know or can't do. Then go ahead and proudly label yourself a geeky girl.

Figure 5. The Idiot Nerd Girl gets something factually incorrect about gamer culture, as the character who wields a sword in *The Legend of Zelda* is actually the hero, Link. By making these newbie mistakes, the Idiot Nerd Girl outs herself as a fake geek girl, someone who is only pretending to be into gaming to impress others. "Idiot Nerd Girl—Image #179,161," *Know Your Meme*, June 8, 2013.

This discourse sets the author up as a true geek girl, one who conforms to a gendered system of power in which most women are suspicious outsiders and only a select few are worthy of being considered an honorary one of the guys—and then only when they go out of their way to disparage a straw woman of their own gender.

The image of the attention-starved fake geek girl is most succinctly captured by the image macro series Idiot Nerd Girl. This meme features a picture of an attractive white girl wearing thick glasses with the word NERD scrawled on her palm. The image is then labeled with a caption of the girl bragging about her love of geeky movies, television shows, and video games. But in the midst of her bragging, she undoes herself by revealing that she doesn't actually know much about the thing she is referencing (Figures 5 and 6). She recognizes that knowledge of geeky texts is necessary to enter gamer culture, but she hasn't actually mastered any of these texts. She can only point to them and hope that this surface-level knowl-

Figure 6. The Idiot Nerd Girl's claim to be a gamer is undermined by her choice of a casual title (*The Sims*), thus making both her an example of a fake geek girl and an example of how masculinity comes to be associated with the hardcore gamer and femininity comes to be associated with the less valued casual gamer. Meme Generator, "gaming? I play the sims sometimes—Idiot Nerd Girl."

edge ingratiates her with the crowd. But her mistakes out her as a poseur. She doesn't deserve gamers' attention because she hasn't put in the work to actually study these texts. Sometimes the captions also purport to reveal the fake geek girl's thought process as she plans to fool a boy into thinking she is a geeky gamer. This version of the meme highlights the fake geek girl's dishonesty, whereas the other highlights her naïveté and her ignorance of gaming culture's most beloved touchstones.

The Idiot Nerd Girl meme generates a background radiation of suspicion as it circulates through gaming culture. Instances of the image macro aren't necessarily directed against a single individual. Instead, they poke fun at a hypothetical class of fake geek girls who supposedly exist out there. This creates an environment in which girls find themselves being carefully watched and tested against the negative example articulated by the meme.

"In Your Subculture, Reappropriating Your Icons"

COUNTERMEMES CAUSING ADDITIONAL GENDER TROUBLE

As these examples show, memetic systems like the gendered system that organizes gaming culture are resilient and flexible, able to adapt to new facts and to label and sort new participants in such a way as to maintain its basic shape even as it is being stretched, questioned, and critiqued. However, because such memes have "polysemic potential," that is, because they have a "tendency to be open to multiple readings" (Shifman 2014, 150), it is possible to use the memetic forms described in this chapter toward different ends. Indeed, a contingent of creators use these memes to stir up additional gender trouble. Michele Knobel and Colin Lankshear call this practice countermemeing, or "the deliberate generation of a meme that aims at neutralizing or eradicating potentially harmful ideas" (2007, 225). Countermemeing seeds the culture with new ideas by smuggling them in using a palatable or familiar vehicle.

For example, in 2012 Rachel Edidin, an editor at Dark Horse Comics, asked her followers on Twitter and Tumblr to "stage a cheerful coup" of the Idiot Nerd Girl meme, using the same image macro to push back against the notion that any girl into gaming culture or geeky culture at large must be a fake (Figure 7). Edidin (n.d.) writes,

> I hate the Idiot Nerd Girl meme because it's not just a meme in the diluted 'net-slang sense. It reflects and recycles and reinforces a bundle of more traditionally defined memes: the sticky and tenacious subtexts and cultural dogmas that justify and normalize misogyny and harassment and make the geek community so seethingly toxic to female members—and especially female newcomers—that it doesn't even need a formal gate to keep them out.[5]

Such countermemes enable their creators to simultaneously signal their ingroup status (as indicated by their familiarity with memetic formats) and their desire to protest that group's social norms through an oppositional or ironic stance.

In Chapter 3, I provide a case study of the kind of struggle that can occur when the gendered memes that thrive in gamer culture (and that often dictate how and which games are made) begin to be challenged from within. I

Figure 7. This meme both describes what the practice of countermemeing does (reappropriating the memetic icons of a subculture and deploying them toward new and potentially politically subversive ends) and what those who circulate the Idiot Nerd Girl meme seem to fear about the entrance of women into gaming culture. From Edidin (2012).

will describe what happens when competing constituencies of video game players vie to define who counts as a member of gaming community, all the while trying to recruit corporate media producers to their cause. Occasionally these struggles result in what looks from the outside like strange alliances, such as one between queer progressive gamers and their allies, who are looking to challenge the gendered hierarchies of gaming culture, and profit-seeking corporations like game developer BioWare, which is trying to figure out how to best pad their bottom line: by going after a narrow band of adolescent straight white male hardcore gamers, or by actively working to broaden their appeal to more diverse demographics at the risk of alienating the hardcore base? This case study provides a model of how to navigate complex systems of power and knowledge in a convergence culture where access to influence over media producers depends directly on whether one is seen as a viable, bankable, reliable consumer.

Game Break

Hacks and Mods

—

REMAKING THE CLASSICS

Hacks and modifications (or mods) are a way for gamers to show off their loyalty toward a favorite franchise (in that they are using their time and labor to extend the gaming experience for themselves and their community), their technical prowess, and the depth of their knowledge of gaming history. Much like their analog cousin, fan fiction, hacks and mods are creative exercises that take place within worlds created by others (Jenkins 1992). They typically feature fan-generated aberrations and adaptations. Game mods might add new features, abilities, or game play modes, or they might change a controversial plot point to better suit the (perceived) desires of the fan base. The latter happened with games like *Final Fantasy 7* (Square, 1997) and *Hate Plus* (Love Conquers All Games, 2013), both of which had a dedicated contingent of fans who refused to accept the scripted deaths of beloved characters and took matters into their own hands, modifying the game to return them to life (Taylor 2011; Hernandez 2014b).

As with all public acts of creation, these hacks and mods are also performances on the part of the author. They posit the existence of a need or a desire in the community and step in to provide for it, thereby assuming a role somewhere in between those of the fan/user and the creator/producer. Given that the performance of the gamer identity is so wrapped up in gendered and sexualized tropes, it is unsurprising that the most popular and commonly known hacks and mods posit a gendered and sexualized identity for their audience: a straight male identity eager (some might say anxious?) to prove itself by subjugating the bodies of women and queer folk.

There is a tendency within modding culture to take strong female characters and render them less intimidating by making them appear in skimpy clothing or even entirely naked. Of course, Lara Croft[1] has been on the receiving end of several nude mods throughout her career as a virtual *Tomb Raider* (Core Design, Eidos Interactive, 1996). However, other games have also had exceedingly popular nude mods, including *Half-Life 2* (Valve Corporation, 2004), *Fallout 3* (Bethesda Game Studios, Bethesda Softworks, 2008), and *The Elder Scrolls V: Skyrim* (Bethesda Game Studios, Bethesda Softworks, 2011) (see Hernandez 2016a). In fact, *Skyrim* and *Tomb Raider* nude mods have been used to generate pornographic machinima[2] videos that have garnered over a million views on a popular pornography website (Hernandez 2015, 2016b).

Hacks of multiplayer online games also take the shape of gendered and sexualized performances. For example, in *Grand Theft Auto Online* (Rockstar Games, 2013), hackers created a script that could take over other people's characters and pose them however they liked. According to Patricia Hernandez (2014a), the mod gave "people the ability to force other players to do things like pole dance and do push-ups. Some modders choose to make other players bend over, and then proceed to use a sex animation from a different part of the game to thrust into them repeatedly, thus making it look like they're raping them. Depending on whether or not the modder has made themselves invincible, victims can't do much in response." However, hacks and mods can also be used to create space within a particular fictional universe for fans who don't feel as though the official canon texts recognize their needs or even their existence.[3] Some modders even manipulate classic old-school video games to make it possible to play as a female protagonist even though the original game does not allow it. For example, game designer Mike Mika (2013) swapped the sprites in *Donkey Kong* (Nintendo, 1981) to make it so that Pauline has to save her boyfriend, Mario; animator Kenna W did the same for Princess Zelda and Link in *The Legend of Zelda* (Nintendo, 1986; Good 2013). Link was also the subject of Mike Hoye's hack of *The Legend of Zelda: Wind Waker* (Nintendo, 2002), though rather than changing out Link's spite, Hoye simply replaced all of Link's pronouns so that the game's text would match his young daughter's assertion that the green-clad hero was a girl.[4] These hackers were working on behalf of a specific audience, sometimes their young daughters and sometimes their past selves, who were "bummed out" that they never got the chance to play as "a magical battle princess that saved her kingdom" (Kenna W 2013)—a princess whom the original version of the game wasn't serving.

However, some hackers project a much larger imagined audience for their work. When Duy Nguyen described why he hacked the farming simulation game *Harvest Moon: Friends of Mineral Town* (Marvelous Interactive, Natsume, 2003) to enable the player character to choose a same-sex partner (in the original game only heterosexual partnerships were possible), he said, "Falling in love is one of the most memorable moments in any Harvest Moon game. Unfortunately for some, it always seemed like you had to choose between who you want to be and who you want to love. I think some of you out there have been waiting for a game like this for a very long time now" (kataiki 2014). Hackers and modders like Nguyen are sometimes viewed by industry professionals as potential bellwethers through which they can catch a glimpse at the desires of the underserved parts of gamer culture. When game designers see that a particular mod is doing exceptionally well, they may include these features in their next official release. According to Julian Kücklich (2005), "Modding is an important source of innovation in the digital games industry. Without the creativity of modders, developers would be hard-pressed to come up with new ideas, and it would prove hard to implement these ideas in the high-risk gaming market were it not for the huge 'test-market' the modding community provides. . . . In effect, the creativity of modders significantly reduces game developers' R&D and marketing costs."

Thus, the creation and dispersal of mods is one way for gamers to prove to developers that their imagined audiences actually exist and are hungry for the type of content that they provide. Unlike Twitter campaigns or news stories about the lack of diversity in games, which industry professionals might write off as manufactured controversies ginned up by nongamers, mods provide hard data to developers about what and how gamers are actually playing; they provide evidence that there is a strong profit motive to create more inclusive games. Indeed, developers seem to be listening:

For example, Nintendo announced a female version of Link, named Linkle, for the game *Hyrule Warriors: Legends* (Koei Tecmo, Team Ninja, Omega Force, 2014; Bolton 2015) Further, the president and CEO of *Harvest Moon* publisher Natsume, Hiro Maekawa, has stated that the company will look into the possibility of including same-sex marriage in future installations of their long-running series, telling reporter Susan Arendt (2014), "We know what the fans are looking for. We are always carefully listening to fans' voices." Hacks and mods are one way that diverse groups of fans are making their voices heard. In Chapter 3, I will look at another case study in fannish activism and the strange alliances that must form to incentivize media producers to create more inclusive content.

No Homosexuals in Star Wars?

BIOWARE, GAMER IDENTITY, AND THE POLITICS OF PRIVILEGE IN A CONVERGENCE CULTURE

N *CONVERGENCE CULTURE*, HENRY JENKINS (2006) lays out a blueprint for participatory culture in which "rather than talking about media producers and consumers as occupying separate roles, we might now see them as participants who interact with each other according to a new set of rules" (3). Jenkins is often read as an optimistic idealist who praises "the promise of this new media environment" to "raise expectations of a freer flow of ideas and content" (18). According to Jenkins, Internet culture grants us all the potential for more democratic, more inclusive mediascapes because corporate media producers will have an economic incentive to listen to the suggestions, requests, and demands made by its audience—and perhaps even to encourage acts of production on the part of users. Therefore, that audience accrues a kind of power to shape and contribute to media production that it has never before wielded so explicitly (62–63).

However, Jenkins is not naive. He points out that "not all participants" in Internet culture "are created equal. . . . Corporations—and even individuals within corporate media—still exert greater power than any individual consumer or even the aggregate of consumers" (2006, 3). He even briefly acknowledges the problem of what he calls the "participation gap," the strong likelihood that "early adopters" and "elite consumers" (who are "disproportionately white, male, middle class, and college educated") will "exert a disproportionate influence on media culture in part because advertisers and media producers are so eager to attract and hold their attention" (23). This is because they are seen as the primary consumers of new media technologies and are therefore thought of as the most desirable target demographic for these products. The perception (or presumption) that new media users are mostly white, male, middle class, college educated, and (although Jenkins does not mention this category) straight leads to a kind of feedback loop that discourages the participation of users who identify with/ as other groups, both because they are not marketed to as potential users and because they risk being labeled as inauthentic participants by their fellows. Despite this admission, however, the majority of Jenkins's book paints media consumers as a relatively unified group standing collectively alongside one another, negotiating with and occasionally entering into conflict with their rival stakeholders in convergence culture: corporations. He often lumps himself, the reader, and the fans he writes about under the pronoun "we," thereby crafting the image of a collective interest group, and he does not spend much time exploring differences among users.

In this chapter, I explore the contours of the participation gap more fully and question who is able to lay claim to titles like "fan" or "gamer"; how those titles are being contested along lines of gender, race, sex, and class; what happens when new users lay claim to those titles; and how some fans are reacting to the loss of their privileged relationships with content producers. I will examine what happens when the channels of communication opened by convergence culture are used to lobby both for and against the inclusion of others, and how the power to influence media production that Jenkins (2006) identifies is being unevenly dispersed and even contested within gamer culture. Media producers watch these interfandom disputes closely so they can determine how to maximize profits. Thus, the outcomes of these squabbles over who and what fans or gamers really are indirectly affect all consumers in the form of mass-produced corporate responses to what exactly it is producers believe their fans want, as dictated by who it is they are convinced their true fans are.

Take, for example, fan responses to BioWare, a North American video game developer, as it attempted to manage discussions of sexuality on their gaming forums. These forums first exploded back in 2009 with a thread about the censorship of terms like "gay" and "lesbian" on the message boards for the MMORPG *Star Wars: The Old Republic* (often abbreviated by gamers as *SW:TOR* or just *TOR*). *TOR* fans argued whether an online gaming forum is an appropriate venue to discuss sexual politics. What was often framed by participants as a benevolent desire to prevent political and ideological conflict from leaking into gaming and ruining its unique attractions wound up ultimately manifesting as a way to maintain a heterocentric power structure. True gamers and fans are assumed to be straight (or, if queer, it is assumed that they will remain in the closet while participating in the gaming forum), and out, queer gamers and their allies are flagged as disruptive and harmful interlopers. This stance implies that BioWare would be doing its "real" fans—the straight male ones they supposedly rely on to sustain their profit margins—a disservice were it to cater to the desires of queer players by making the forum community queer friendly. A similar debate arose two years later when BioWare made the decision to include gay romance options in their popular single-player role-playing game franchise, *Dragon Age*. Again, a subset of forum participants argued that including queer romances would be a waste of BioWare's resources, better devoted to serving hardcore gamers. The idea that hardcore gamers might enjoy queer romantic story lines was, in their minds, inconceivable.

Ultimately, for both games, BioWare decided that the business they stood to gain from explicitly reaching out to and including game elements requested by queer players and their allies would outweigh the business they stood to lose from straight male fans who were upset at losing their privileged status as the sole demographic game developers aimed to please. This scenario complicates the usual positions of corporations and users in accounts of convergence culture, where users are assumed to be a homogenous group pushing for more inclusive, more democratic, more open media environments, and corporations are assumed to be reluctantly capitulating to the virtuous demands of the enlightened masses.

A Short History of Censorship and Queerness on the BioWare Forums

BioWare's gay-mer troubles first began in April 2009, when news of a new thread on the message boards for *TOR* spread like wildfire through the gaming blogosphere. These message boards give fans a place to gather and discuss press releases, form cooperative gaming groups called guilds, and offer suggestions to developers about possible directions the game might take. They are also regulated by moderators to ensure that discussions remain civil and family friendly. To this end, the moderators on the *TOR* forum developed and announced an automatic filter that looked for certain words deemed inappropriate. This verboten language included the words "gay" and "lesbian" (Sliwinski 2009).

It is true that the word "gay" is notoriously used throughout the gaming world (Cole 2009) "to describe anything unmasculine, non-normative, or uncool" (Thurlow 2001, 26) (see also Chapter 1), and the reasoning behind BioWare's ban on these words may have been aimed at curtailing derogatory uses of the term. Other gaming entities like Blizzard Entertainment and Microsoft had instituted similar policies around such words in the past, even going so far as to ban players who were up front about their own sexual orientations, telling them that it was for their own protection (Ward 2006; Gilbert 2009). However, shortly after BioWare's linguistic ban was put in place, a poster nicknamed Elikal started one of many threads on the message board asking the company to reconsider the censoring of these terms (Elikal). Among the several concerns raised on Elikal's thread (which was by far the longest-lasting and most popular thread on this topic) was the notion that such "solutions" only help to further marginalize the gay and lesbian community, making it difficult for gay and lesbian players to find each other online by labeling the identities they have chosen for themselves "taboo" or "dirty" (Fdzzaigl 2009). For example, a poster named Kevar argued, "A minority requesting that they be represented in a game that is entirely about developing the identity of your character requires loudness. If they don't make their voices heard, BioWare doesn't see the demand, and it doesn't go in the game" (Kevar 2009). Sherle_Illios (2009) took a similar tack, writing, "One cannot open up a world for players to play/live/communicate/tell their stories in and expect these [words such as 'gay' and 'lesbian'] to *not* exist in it." These gamers are arguing that it is the forcible closeting of queer players, not the visibility of queer users, that politicizes the game space. On the other hand, many posters jumped onto the thread and defended BioWare's decision, arguing that discussions of gay and lesbian issues are irrelevant to the stated purpose of the forums: talking about the forthcoming game. Ultimately BioWare decided to reinstate the ability of posters to use these words in the wake of the attention the controversy garnered in the gaming press.

This incident is an ideal case study of the political and social dynamics in online gaming communities because the thread in question was widely viewed both within the *TOR* forum and in the larger gaming community via news sites like *Kotaku* and *Destructoid*. It eventually even got some attention from outside gaming circles when Tony Perkins's conservative group Focus on the Family covered the "biggest threat to the Empire" posed by "homosexual activists" (Good 2012). (Apparently Perkins did not realize that in the Star Wars universe, the Empire is evil.) Despite its location in an out-of-the-way, unpopular corner of the forums (the unexciting and utilitarian Website Feedback and Support board on the General Discussion forum), this thread accumulated over 1,200 posts and tens of thousands of views—exposure comparable to that of the most popular sticky threads (that is, threads with important information that are always located at the top of the forum and are never bumped off the front page by new threads), or to the extremely popular official threads offering previews of in-game content. This fact attests to the importance accorded to the debate by community members, regardless of which side they found themselves on.

Will the Real Gamers Please Stand Up?

STRAIGHT PRIVILEGE ONLINE

One faction of gamers defended BioWare's decision to censor the terms "gay" and "lesbian" by arguing that there should be a stark divide between the game space and the outside world, and that political language about sexual identity undermines that division. Vili Lehdonvirta (2010) critiques this position, arguing that it mistakenly imagines virtual worlds as "located outside 'the real world,' in many ways mirroring it like a synthetic double, but carrying on independently of it like a distant planet." To Lehdonvirta, the real and the virtual are inseparable. Gamers cannot help but bring their real-world selves with them into the game, and vice versa. Indeed, as people of all stripes find their jobs and their social lives increasingly mediated by the Internet, it is becoming difficult to argue that virtual interactions are not real, impactful parts of our everyday lives.

However, the gamers described here are dedicated to the idea of a virtual world as a space apart, a magic circle much like the one described by cultural historian Johan Huizinga (1955)—a space set aside for playful experiences free from real-world consequences. These gamers consider any attempts to pierce the barrier between the virtual world and the real world as a threat to their enjoyment of the game. According to their view, the introduction of real-world political concerns into the digital world disrupts the barrier they've tried to erect between their time in *TOR* and the rest of their day-to-day existence. They thus argued that BioWare should help them maintain that barrier, insisting that there is no place for progressive political activism, or indeed any overtly political speech, in a space that has been set aside for play.[1]

These gamers desire (and expect) the erasure of political rhetoric within virtual worlds. They do not simply abstain from themselves mixing the real with the virtual. They also scold others for doing so out in the open where they can be seen, turning such world mixing into a social faux pas, an indicator that one is not truly a citizen of utopian Internet space. In the case of *TOR*, that scolding was reserved for those who protested against BioWare's decision to ban the words "gay" and "lesbian" on their forums. The implication was that the forum members who raised those concerns must not be real game fans, and so their concerns could and should be ignored by game producers like BioWare when they crafted rules for the forum.

One popular rhetorical tactic was to accuse protesters of hijacking the thread, posting something off topic for the forum in question. These accusations were common even though the subject under consideration in the thread was the rules governing the forum, not some broader political subject matter. In addition, the thread was correctly housed in the Website Feedback and Support board and not on one of the boards about game play topics. Such accusations carry some weight in that, according to BioWare's rules of conduct, "discussions of political, sexual, or religious topics are prohibited on the forums" and "posts deemed to be inappropriate to a particular forum will be moved to a more appropriate forum or removed completely" ("Rules of Conduct" 2011). In other words, these arguments carry the threat of moderator intervention, perhaps even a ban. They suggest an alignment of purpose between BioWare and the accuser, who poses as someone attempting to helpfully enforce the forum's code of conduct.

This attempt to draft forum authorities into seeing things their way (or to stand in for them) creates a social environment in which queer-identified users and their allies are read as guilty subjects. Moreover, the argument that gaming while (out and) queer is harmful to the community represents an attempt to recruit queer gamers into seeing themselves as guilty so that they will self-censor. The ultimate aim is to divest gamers who insist on bringing queerness into the game world of cultural capital by questioning their gamer bona fides, thereby ensuring that queer issues receive little attention from game producers and that the status quo of gamer culture is maintained. Many gamers took a similar position to the one espoused by punkniner (2009a): "This is quite possibly the dumbest thing I have ever seen argued about on a video gaming forum. Congratulations. If you want to protest, go to your town hall. The simple fact is, this is a forum about a video game, and there is no purpose whatsoever to bring up this kind of nonsense."[2] In a later post, punkniner (2009b) takes this point even further and declares that all political discussions are out of place on the *TOR* forums: "This is a forum about a Star Wars video game. Will we now be arguing and complaining over abortion rights, or even the presidential election? I'm sure we can somehow tie those into a star wars theme somewhere (Palpatine was elected by a majority vote just like Bush!), and they are just as pointless and off base from the subject matter as the argument set forth in this thread." To gamers like punkniner, any attempt to lobby for a more inclusive stance toward queerness is understood to be an attempt to rudely divert discussion away from the game itself and toward what is perceived as a personal, political agenda—something a real gamer would supposedly never do.

Leaving the Body Behind

IDENTITY POLITICS AND TECHNOUTOPIAN THEORY

Importantly, the political discussion in question is not centered on just any controversial issue but rather is focused on issues of embodiment, identity, and privilege. This thread about the suppression of queerness in *TOR* drew a great deal of attention from players because it taps into how elite participants in gaming culture view their relationship to media producers: they assume that their influence is a finite resource, and they dislike the idea that their privilege within gaming culture could be diluted as gaming expands in popularity.

Participants in the thread sought to protect what they saw as their own privileged position by tapping into another prominent thread of technoutopian thinking: that on the Internet, the bodies and identities that we were born with are irrelevant (Adam 2002, 159; Stone 2000, 113). Their belief that the virtual world is a world freed from the constraints of the physical body is in no small part the way technophiles provide evidence for their claim that the virtual and the real are or can be separated in the first place.

This claim is usually couched in hopeful terms; it is used to explain how the new social order created online will be free of the scourges of racism, sexism, homophobia, and ableism. Discrimination, or so the argument goes, will be impossible when users are unable to see the actual bodies of those with whom they are interacting. (For more on this, see the Introduction.)

This is essentially the claim being made by many gamers on the *TOR* thread: that BioWare was simply protecting the sanctity of the disembodied and anonymous virtual culture when they set up rules that would eliminate references to queer sexualities. This claim is threaded through the argument of poster LordByrondathird (2009):

> now i don't mean this to be offensive, and i see your point. it's totally legit. but like one person already said, this is about star wars, and its fans. Its not about who's what orientation, or religion, or race or gender. if so, you might be hearing a lot more pro islam, or pro christian, or pro life, or pro feminism and so on. again, i see your point, but this is about star wars. Im sure there's a lot of people like you on here, just like there's plenty of religious people, or femenists, but we're all here because of our love of star wars and The Old Republic.

At the core of LordByrondathird's post is the idea that discussions of politics and sexuality are unwelcome in the discourse space that this poster believes is reserved for "our love of star wars" in that they corrupt the purity of a space he or she believes should exist separately from such issues.[3] Furthermore, according to LordByrondathird, one of the primary ways in which unsavory politics are introduced into the game world is when one is able to identify "who's what orientation . . . or race or gender." When physical embodiment returns, this argument goes, it brings politics with it.

Indeed, the idea that any discussion related to embodied sexuality (straight or queer) is unwelcome on the forums and in the game comes up numerous times in the thread. A comment from indelible (2009), quoted here at length, complains that "personal" and divisive issues like sexuality cause unnecessary divisions within the Star Wars fan community. Indelible then accuses those who would bring sexual politics into the game space of the virtual equivalent of disturbing the peace:

> I'm inclined to say that—on an online gaming forum—your sexuality is of no concern to anyone else. I'm not going to ask you and frankly,

I really couldn't care less. I'm here for the game. I'm not here to have people tell me whether they are lesbian, gay or straight or to start any debates about equality. . . .

You have brought that conflict and imposed it on a group of people who—for all intents and purposes—transcended the whole issue in the first place. . . . There is no war on these forums that you haven't brought on yourself with this thread. If people start attacking gays and lesbians, it is simply because you have drawn attention to the issue which—in all reality—didn't need attention drawn to it within this community. . . .

I'm sorry—I understand you struggle for equality and empathy in the real world, where that sort of issue is important—but here, on a gaming forum . . . it just isn't the right time or place for a political debate and it certainly isn't the place to encourage some kind of social change, mainly because many of us could give a flying hoot who or what you sleep with.

Of particular interest is indelible's claim that discrimination has been "transcended" in the bodiless virtual world. This enlightenment must be precarious if it can only be sustained when gamers enact a "don't ask, don't tell" policy regarding their sexual orientations. Indelible is claiming that gamers who reintroduce the body into virtual spaces by making their sexuality visible are to blame for any abuse that they receive, as that abuse would never have happened if the wider community was allowed to remain blissfully unaware of the presence of queers in their midst.

Furthermore, requests like those made by indelible to censor any references to sexual orientation (including heterosexual orientations) would not actually open up space for users to quietly be queer online. Rather, as theorists of the body like Susan Bordo (2003) have pointed out, the disappearance of queerness would simply reinforce the assumption of universal straightness among gamers and forum dwellers. Bordo describes the way in which a splitting off of the mind from the body such as the one that technoutopians assume takes place when we go online has historically been used as a philosophical rationalization for the maintenance of a hierarchical social organization that privileges straight white able-bodied men (2003, 2–5). According to this logic, the body itself comes to be seen a site that is feminized, racialized, sexualized, and/or disabled (9), while the "'generic' core" of identity that is supposed to pass as genderless, raceless, sexless, and bodiless (the soul, the mind, the human essence) comes to be read as "white or male . . . passing as the norm for all" (34). This means that women, queers, racial minorities, and disabled persons have bodies that call attention to themselves through their marked differentness from the supposedly normal bodies of straight white able-bodied men. Meanwhile, citizens with generic bodies—the straight white able-bodied men whose place at the top of the social hierarchy means that their bodies are the bodies to which all others are compared and judged to be deficient (or at the very least noteworthy)—are thought to come close to the ideal of disembodiedness (Dyer 1997, 1–2).

Michael Warner describes the inscription of this process with regards to sexuality as heteronormativity: the assumption that straightness is universal and all-encompassing, and that queerness is an aberration or an outlying position created by privileging straightness over queerness (1993, xxi). According to this (often invisible) cultural framework, straight culture is seen as normal, natural, and nonideological, while queer culture is seen as aberrant, artificial, and hyperpoliticized. In the virtual world, heteronormativity takes the form of what Jenny Sundén calls "heterotextuality," the assumption that all users (as represented by the texts they write online) are straight in the absence of any mention of sexuality (2003, 130–31). This assumption is only discarded when users directly out themselves as queer—a practice that allows the body to return and thereby may draw the ire of technoutopian users looking to escape bodies and their politics. Heterotextuality is thus one example of the many ways that users discipline identity formation in online spaces to secure the fantasy of a virtual realm free from difference and therefore free from political conflict. Queerness is erased in favor of a universal silent sameness (which is ultimately read as straightness). Users who insist on reintroducing the existence of queerness into the game space are derided as agitators, bringing unnecessary turmoil into what was (for users who conform to the norm) a pleasantly placid environment. The dislocation felt by queer users in the face of great pressures to remain closeted online are not taken into consideration. Instead, queer users are asked to put off their concerns for the sake of the comfort of larger group. Their insistence that their communities be accepting of queer sexualities in practice, not merely tolerated so long as they are kept safely out of sight, is perceived as a kind of buzzkill, a disruption of the benevolent fantasy that the denizens of online communities have transcended bodily matters.

It thus becomes apparent that the rallying cry of "no politics in gaming" actually has huge political consequences within the gamer community. As Althusser (1972) points out, "ideology" or "politics" is always the label given to what someone else cares about. People think of their own concerns as rational and logical, and they assume that it is only others who are motivated by politics or tricked by ideology. This is what makes ideology so durable: it is difficult to see when it is operating on you. In the case of this debate in the gaming community, heteronormative ideology disguises itself as the rational default position of loyal gamers, while those who lobby for the inclusion of queerness are labeled as ideologically driven political operatives. This labeling functions to disguise the heterosexist ideological constraints that portray straightness as the normal, natural, default human state in the first place.

BioWare Strikes Back

CORPORATE RESPONSES ENCOURAGING DIVERSITY IN THE NAME OF PROFIT

These same discourses arose again in BioWare's online forums in the wake of the implementation of gay relationships for male player characters in the single-player *Dragon Age* franchise (Kuchera 2011). This time, some gamers were explicit and direct about expressing their ire with BioWare for being willing to, as they saw it, dilute the influence of their "core demographic" (Bastal 2011) of straight male gamers by producing more inclusive games. In March 2011, a poster named Bastal responded to the developer's choice to include these queer narratives on the Official Campaign Quests and Story board of the BioWare Social Network forums by creating multiple threads with slight variations on the same name: "BioWare Neglected Their Main Demographic: The Straight Male Gamer." Bastal chided *Dragon Age II* (BioWare, Electronic Arts, 2011) developers for including queer content in the game using many of the same old arguments based on techno-utopianism and antiembodiment.[4]

Bastal (2011) begins his[5] argument with the assumption that straightness and maleness is universal and normal when he opens his post: "I don't think many would argue with the fact that the overwhelming majority of RPG gamers are indeed straight and male." He continues, "its ridiculous that I even have to use a term like Straight Male Gamer, when in the past I would only have to say fans." He soon reveals that he does not merely feel as though the desires of his particular demographic of the straight male gamer have been neglected. He also argues that the mere inclusion of the option to partake in queer content is an affront to him as a straight male gamer. To this end, he calls for a "'No Homosexuality' option" to be implemented in the game so that he can be certain that his personal version of the fantasy setting of Thedas would be free from the incursion of queerness.

Dragon Age II senior writer David Gaider (2011) responded directly to Bastal with a lengthy post rejecting the argument that there should be an option to eradicate gays and lesbians from one's personal copy of the game world. First, Gaider rejects the assumption that all or even most gamers are straight: "The romances in the game are not for 'the straight male gamer.' They're for everyone. We have a lot of fans, many of whom are neither straight nor male, and they deserve no less attention. We have good numbers, after all, on the number of people who actually used similar sorts of content . . . and thus don't need to resort to anecdotal evidence to support our idea that their numbers are not insignificant." Even more to the point, Gaider notes that rather than eliminating political concerns by erasing queerness, such requests actually inject a politics of privilege and hierarchy into the game:

> And if there is any doubt why such an opinion might be met with hostility, it has to do with privilege. You can write it off as "political correctness" if you wish, but the truth is that privilege always lies with the majority. They're so used to being catered to that they see the lack of catering as an imbalance. They don't see anything wrong with having things set up to suit them, what's everyone's fuss all about? That's the way it should be, and everyone else should be used to not getting what they want.

This thread demonstrates movement on the issue of inclusion in the gaming community, in part fueled by the feedback BioWare received from queer gamers and their allies during the debate over *TOR*. Furthermore, Gaider's decision to respond to the post in the first place suggests a responsiveness to user input that is an important feature of convergence culture. However, it is important to note that this responsiveness is directed toward the desires of one group of users and against the desires of another. This complication runs counter to typical accounts of convergence culture in which fandom is portrayed as a single united entity working with (or against) media corporations to further their own interests as consumers. In this case, inclusive, democratic outcomes to the question of whether to implement queer content were made possible because BioWare's profit motive coincided with the expressed desires of some users, though the company risked the ire of other users when they made their decision. This outcome was not some foregone conclusion, one predetermined by the technological affordances of new media and convergence culture.

BioWare eventually implemented queer content in *TOR* after fans mounted a sustained campaign for what they called same-gender romances, or SGRs. However, the content came with a twin set of prices attached. First, the content was released as a part of an expansion pack that costs players an additional fee to access (thus demonstrating the necessity of there being the potential for profitability for a gaming company to act). Second, the update confines all of the queer romanceable characters to a single planet in the *TOR* universe called Makeb (Hamilton 2013). When considered together, these two developments seem to represent a compromise on the part of BioWare developers between those fans who are calling for queer content and those demanding it be kept out. Under this system, players like Bastal who want their Star Wars universe to remain for straight folks need only refrain from purchasing the expansion. Furthermore, this setup posits the "straight" version of that universe as the default version. The presence of queerness is thus constructed as an unnecessary add-on, a bonus that fans can pay for if they are so inclined, but not an essential part of the world being co-constructed by players and game developers. In addition, players who want the other additional content contained in the expansion (which also extended the level cap for player characters and extended the game's story line) could feel reassured that it would be easy to avoid even accidentally running into a queer NPC. All they had to do was refrain from visiting Makeb, which critics quickly began to refer to as *TOR*'s "gay ghetto planet" (Pearson 2013). This dual system of segregation (economic and spatial) demonstrates the problematic compromises that are produced by the interactions between fans and creators.

As these events demonstrate, convergence culture enables much more complex relationships between users and producers to develop than was previously thought. Various factions of elite users who recognize and seize the power to talk back to media corporations through the channels opened up by the development of a convergence culture are not merely lobbying to see their own interests reflected in the media they consume, thereby creating a more democratic and inclusive media environment. They are also using those same channels to try and protect what they see as their privileged position within the convergence culture, to the extent that they fear that the efforts of media corporations to broaden their fan base will dilute their power. If we fail to include schisms like these in our account of how convergence culture is developing, then that account will be woefully inadequate to accurately model power sharing in the world of new media.

Game Break

Will the Circle Be Unbroken?

—

BIOSHOCK INFINITE AND THE EVOLUTION
OF HARDCORE GAMING CULTURE

rrational Games and Ken Levine's *BioShock* (2K Games, 2007) series is well known among video game fans and critics for its metadiscursive references to gaming tropes. The original game in the series is a first-person shooter set in the underwater city of Rapture, an objectivist paradise that has descended into ruin and civil war. The player character, a man named Jack from our world above the water, is involved in a plane crash and stumbles on the city in the midst of the chaos. He is contacted via radio by a revolutionary named Atlas, who requests Jack's help in overthrowing Andrew Ryan, the city's founder. However, about midway through the game, the story turns on its head when it is revealed that Atlas is actually the nefarious Frank Fontaine, a con man and a criminal who has brainwashed Jack into serving as a weapon against Ryan. Using the trigger phrase "Would you kindly . . . ," Fontaine is able to direct Jack's progress through the city by mind control. Within the diegetic world of the plot, all of the actions that Jack believed that he performed of his own free will were actually being chosen by someone else.

As entertaining and horrifying as this plot twist is on a narrative level, it also serves as a kind of commentary on the actions of the players, who until this point were able to indulge in the pleasant fantasy that they were choosing a unique path through a living game world. However, as one scene cleverly demonstrates, the path through the game has been predetermined for the players: "In a crucial point of the game *BioShock* a cut scene occurs and the player watches while the avatar performs a vicious action because the game, not the player, tells it to. . . . And in that moment, much of the illusion of control that a player has over the game experience is laid bare" (Wysocki and Schandler 2013, 200). Gamers describe this kind of predestination as being "on rails": much like a train, players may be strong and powerful, but they can only travel along a preset track. They must move through the city, collecting items and abilities that enable them to advance, killing enemies and bosses as they present themselves, or the game does not go forward. The game provides only the illusion of control. In actuality, players act out a script that has been written for them beforehand.

"A man chooses," Ryan admonishes Jack; "a slave obeys." *BioShock* trains the player to imagine himself or herself as "the man" going about manly, heroic business. But the player is actually a "slave" to the games programming.

> The "Would you kindly?" scene can cause us to question all of our motivation and activity in gaming up to this point. Why is it suddenly upsetting that we are "killing" this "individual" yet we, if not happily, at least agreeably slaughtered dozens, if not hundreds, of other characters to get to this point, some of them potentially virtual children in the form of the Little Sisters? Yet now we wish to not be complicit in the killing of Andrew Ryan. Where were the protests and frustrations prior to this? (Wysocki and Schandler 2013, 205)

Although Jack seemingly does get his free will back after this scene is concluded and Fontaine has been revealed, the player does not. The game remains on rails. The player still has to jump through the game's scripted hoops to progress, moving toward the inevitable final boss fight: "No other options present themselves. No other choices may be made. The player cannot attempt to make peace with Fontaine . . . or even just flee Rapture on their own" (Wysocki and Schandler 2013, 206). According to Jessica Aldred and Brian Greenspan, "*BioShock* allegorizes the procedures through which gamers are compelled to purchase converged devices despite their planned obsolescence, consume converged content in the order and fashion desired by media producers, and accept that the choices and agency they are given are illusory at best" (2011, 482).

INFINITE REFLECTIONS

If the first game in the *BioShock* series is a reflection upon the philosophical implications of on-rails game play/storytelling mechanics, then its sequel, *BioShock Infinite* (Irrational Games, 2K Games, 2013), is a reflection on the social makeup of gaming culture writ large. In particular, the game takes the subculture to task for turning inward in an attempt to maintain its exclusivity, suggesting that this inward turn has led gaming as an art form into a rut. It can only escape, it seems, if the oft retold tropes about gender, race, and empire that dominate video game storytelling are overthrown in favor of new stories featuring new kinds of characters and new perspectives.

Bioshock Infinite is set in Columbia, a city suspended among the clouds. Like Rapture, the city is wondrous at first glance, with a quaint nineteenth-century feeling to its architecture and to the clothes worn by its population that conveys a sense of innocence and simplicity. One might even say that the community looks Edenic, which is appropriate because its founder, Zachary Comstock, is a Christian religious leader and self-described prophet. However, shortly after the player's arrival in the city as Booker DeWitt (a private detective who has been hired to rescue a girl named Elizabeth), it becomes clear that there is something awful going on beneath Columbia's beautiful surface. Columbia is actually a hotbed of racism and segregation; the comfort and beauty of the city is only made possible by the exploitation and exclusion of people of color.

Columbia is an allegorical representation of the Internet in general and of gaming culture in particular. The city was founded as an attempt at a utopian community separate from the mundane, everyday world. Its separation from the world below was made possible through the application of technology. In this Columbia's founders mimic the technoutopian goals of early Internet pioneers. However, much like the gamers I describe in this book, its residents not only wound up reinstantiating the prejudices of the world they left behind but they also developed and refined them so that they might better fit the logics that governed their insular community. Furthermore, like its predecessor, *BioShock Infinite* references numerous video game tropes, combining and remixing archetypal images, characters, and tasks that have been recycled throughout gaming history. For example, Booker's initial mission, like hundreds of game heroes from Super Mario to Earthworm Jim before him (see Sarkeesian 2013a, 2013b), is to rescue Elizabeth, the "princess" of Columbia. Indeed, early in the game, Elizabeth looks rather like a Disney princess, with her exaggeratedly large eyes, tiny waist, innocent demeanor, and tendency to sing and dance when delighted.

As soon as Booker busts Elizabeth out of her imprisonment, another standard video game mission begins: the escort mission. An escort mission is a game type wherein a player must follow and protect a nonplayable character (NPC) governed by the game's artificial intelligence, shepherding the character to a safe location. Escortees are typically much weaker than the player character/hero, and they are often either damsels in distress (Sarah 2013) or children. A classic escort mission NPC is someone like the president's daughter in *Resident Evil 4* (Capcom, 2005), or a female scientist who complains that your guns are too loud as you are guarding her life in *GoldenEye 007* (Nintendo, 1997). In *BioShock Infinite*, Elizabeth's escort mission is typical in some ways and atypical in others. Like most escorted NPCs, Elizabeth will not fight alongside you. Even though Elizabeth harbors the power to radically alter time and space, her function in relation to the player character is purely one of support (see Chapter 2). She will scrounge for bullets, healing items, and money; occasionally she will pick locks or clear the way to new areas, but she refuses to join you in battle as you fight your way clear of Columbia, and she often chides you for being so violent. On the other hand, unlike the damsels found in most escort missions, Elizabeth is no fainting flower. She never shrieks or dissolves into tears when the fighting breaks out. Instead, the game explicitly tells the player, "You don't need to protect Elizabeth in combat. She can take care of herself." This allows the player to invest more fully in her as a character instead of being frustrated by her as an object to be pushed through the game's environment.

But if Elizabeth inspired devotion from fans of the game as a unique and likable character, Booker, the player's avatar in the world of *Bioshock Infinite*, is much less compelling. He is a "Generic, Grizzled, White [male video game] Protagonist" (Gregar 2014) of the type that has become ubiquitous in recent years (Concelmo 2010), a "run-of-the-mill white guy with no personality or flavor" (Hinkley 2012). Indeed, the box art for the game, which features Booker scowling at the player and holding a gun, was widely criticized as being overly "generic," a stale "*Call of Duty* imitation" that fails to capture the unique flavor of the game's steampunk setting (Kain 2012).

The game mechanics the player uses to control Booker are also recycled from games past: specifically earlier games in the *BioShock* series. Most of the weapons and upgrades are simply what we might call reskins—that is, they are aesthetically different to match the new setting but functionally the same—of those that you would find in Rapture, the underwater city featured in the first two games. In addition, the game's setting, an all but inaccessible technological antiutopia led by a charismatic leader, is reminiscent of Rapture.

However, this video game déjà vu is not simply laziness on the part of the game's programmers. It foreshadows the game world's final reveal, and the biggest metadiscursive twist in the history of a franchise famous for them. When Booker finally destroys the tower that had been imprisoning Elizabeth, the full measure of her power is released, and her control over space and time becomes complete. It is then revealed that the *BioShock* games, which had previously seemed to be related only in terms of play style and not in terms of plot, actually take place in the same universe. Or rather, they take place within the same multiverse—one composed of infinite adjacent universes, all slightly different from the ones next door. Each universe has the same major constants: a lighthouse through which one enters a fallen utopian city, a man at its helm who has gone mad with power, the little girls that they exploit, and a brewing revolution that will plunge the city into violence and chaos. However, each universe also features several variables, minor differences that distinguish them. In one universe, a tyrant uses religion as an excuse to reject the fallen world. In another, a tycoon rationalizes his rejection of altruism and charity by founding a city on the principles of objectivism. *BioShock*'s city under the sea and *BioShock Infinite*'s city in the clouds are parallel: the same story plays out in each city, across every city in the multiverse: one in which one group or another (women, people of color, queer folk, the poor) are treated as tools at best or as target practice (literally) at worst. In such a world, it makes sense that Booker would be a generic protagonist, someone that players could encounter across any number of video games, because that is exactly what he is. He is but one version of a million grizzled, brown-haired white men with guns found in a million stories, each of which unfold in more or less the same way.

This multiverse, with its many readily apparent recycled gaming tropes, is a metaphor for an increasingly stagnant pool of AAA games. Video games and virtual worlds are supposed to be able to transport us to thousands of unique and exciting new worlds. However, because the marketplace for games is thought to belong to only a narrow sliver of young straight white male hardcore gaming enthusiasts, the sum of the worlds created by AAA games simply repeatedly retells the same stories but in slightly different locales. We might imagine the entirety of gaming history contained within Elizabeth's sea of lighthouses. This should give us pause, for these parallel universes differ only by degree, not kind. They only enable players to experience a particular kind of fantasy over and over again. Furthermore, as a result of the imagined homogenization of the consumer base for these games, those stories tend to treat the kind of people who are thought to be outside of the target demographic as mere props: prizes to be rescued or bodies to kill in an ever-renewable orgy of violence.

However, *Bioshock Infinite* does have something unique in Elizabeth, who ultimately realizes that the only way to truly undo the violence and misery caused by Comstock in the city of Columbia is to erase it from the multiverse altogether—to travel back to the point at which the crucial decision that led to Comstock's birth was made and "smother him in his crib." After all, Elizabeth is able to see all possible worlds and all possible futures in each of the universes within the multiverse. Thus, it is not enough for her to end Comstock's reign in her world. He must be stopped in all worlds. In the game's final twist, it is revealed that Booker and Comstock are actually the same man from different parallel universes, representing two different paths taken after one crucial decision. Elizabeth realizes that the only way to keep Comstock from appearing anywhere in space and time is to kill Booker at the point in time when that decision was made. It is implied that by doing so, Elizabeth will erase the events that took place within *Bioshock Infinite* from history—or rather from all possible histories. The only way to make room for new kinds of stories is to clear away the old ones. Booker's truest act of heroism is when he sacrifices himself to allow for the creation of a better world where people like Elizabeth can step forward and lead.

BURIAL AT SEA

Just as *Bioshock Infinite* at first seemed to be entirely unconnected to earlier games in the series, the *Bioshock Infinite* downloadable content expansion/sequel, *Burial at Sea*, initially seems to have little to obviously connect it to its predecessor. In fact, it looks like a bizarre conflation of elements from both the earlier *Bioshock* games and *Bioshock Infinite*. In *Episode 1* (Irrational Games, 2K Games, 2013), you still play as Booker, but instead of Columbia, you live in Rapture, the underwater Ayn Rand–ian paradise from the original *Bioshock*. An older version of Elizabeth, decked out as a film noir femme fatale, hires Booker to find Sally, a little orphaned girl who has gone missing. Booker fears that Sally might have been turned into a Little Sister, one of a troop of girls whose special powers are exploited to keep Rapture running (a mirror of the way that Elizabeth's powers were used in Columbia).

On their way to rescue Sally, Booker and Elizabeth encounter Frank Fontaine as he prepares to start his revolution against city founder Andrew Ryan—the very revolution that is the backdrop for the first game in the series. They do succeed in finding Sally and are horrified to discover that she has been turned into a Little Sister. However, at the end of *Episode 1*, the player discovers that Elizabeth had no interest in Sally at all. Instead, she was using Sally (whom Booker was fond of) as bait to find this universe's incarnation of Booker/Comstock, who escaped the destruction of all his other incarnations by fleeing from Columbia to Rapture. When she kills this final version of Booker, Elizabeth feels as though her revenge on the man who destroyed her life across multiple worlds is finally complete.

Episode 2 (Irrational Games, 2K Games, 2014) thus begins with the player controlling Elizabeth instead of Booker. However, Elizabeth is horrified to realize that in using Sally as an instrument in her revenge, she has perpetuated the cycle of destruction that she sought to end. She rid the multiverse of one violent and exploitative dictator, only to step into his place. She thus decides to make things right by returning to Rapture and making a new choice: she will rescue Sally instead of leaving her to her fate as a Little Sister. Unfortunately, in order to return, Elizabeth must collapse her multidimensional self into a regular old mortal. She gives up her powers and her ability to see into the future, and sets herself on a path to pay off her own debt to Sally—a path that will ultimately lead to her own death.

In making Elizabeth the player's avatar, *Burial at Sea* finishes the work begun by *Bioshock Infinite*. Now that all of the versions of generic gun-toting hero Booker/Comstock have been cleared away, a new story can be told about new characters—ones who realize the mistakes of their predecessors and strive to do something different, to be better. The expansion even uses new game mechanics to illustrate this shift in what the central character values. Rather than solving every problem by direct assault, Elizabeth prefers to take a stealthy approach: she hides from her opponents and knocks them unconscious with a blow to the head or a tranquilizer dart. (A nice detail: you can hear them breathing after she knocks them out, and you can see their chests rising and falling.) Furthermore, if the player chooses to participate in one of the easier game modes, Elizabeth can fall back on guns if she runs out of options. However, in the most difficult play mode, the game removes this option, thus making the least violent method the most hardcore for those gamers invested in demonstrating their elite skills ("Announcing 1998 Mode" 2014).

Burial at Sea even uses its time-traveling story line to go back and make the previous games in the *Bioshock* series more inclusive by retconning the story of the original game. "Retcon" stands for "retroactive continuity," a process by which a creator "retrofits the series . . . by means of a revisionary view of past events" (Denson 2013, 277). By intervening in events in Rapture, Elizabeth retrofits herself into its history (and thus into *Bioshock*'s series history). Unbeknownst to us, it was really she who set into motion the events of the first game by giving Atlas the activation phrase he uses to control Jack. Because of her ability to glimpse the future, Elizabeth knows that, far from handing Atlas to key to his own victory, she is actually sowing the seeds of his future destruction and setting the scene for Jack to rescue the Little Sisters, thus finally ending the cycle of violence in Rapture as well as Columbia. This act of retconning recasts the *Bioshock* series by making Elizabeth's choice, not Jack's or Booker's, the crux of the overall narrative. Her choice makes Jack's heroism possible. *Burial at Sea* retroactively enables a multiplication of voices within one of the most revered titles in gaming culture, creating new viewpoints from which to view the artifacts of that culture.

Episode 2 of *Burial at Sea* also retcons another important character from *Bioshock Infinite*, one whom many thought had been given a raw deal by her original story line. Daisy Fitzroy is the leader of the Vox Populi, a resistance group dedicated to bringing down Comstock's racist and classist regime. In *Bioshock Infinite*, many gamers were frustrated by the midgame twist in which Fitzroy threatens to kill the innocent child of one of Columbia's leaders, thereby forcing Elizabeth to kill her. Critics such as Elizabeth Maffetone (2013) were frustrated by Fitzroy's story line because it seemingly played into a narrative around race and racism in which "both sides" (racists and their victims) are depicted as equally irrational and equally culpable for their society's ills. However, *Episode 2* retcons Daisy's story by allowing Elizabeth to travel back to Columbia and glimpse the lead-up to this fateful moment. Elizabeth discovers that another pair of time travelers with powers like her own, the Lutece twins, actually convinced Daisy to threaten the child against her will. Just as Elizabeth had foreseen both the positive and the negative consequences of her decision to return to Rapture (the liberation of the Little Sisters and her own death, respectively), the Luteces foresaw that the downfall of Columbia could only happen once Elizabeth lost her innocence. Daisy's decision to sacrifice herself in order to ensure that someone else was able to complete her task mirrors Booker's decision to sacrifice himself to save Columbia, as well as Elizabeth's decision to sacrifice herself to save Sally and the other Little Sisters. Yet Daisy's sacrifice is even greater, considering that, unlike Elizabeth, she couldn't be certain of the future that her sacrifice was bringing about. Once again, the downloadable content expands the scope of the original game to include different types of heroism and different types of heroes than it is possible to imagine in the original.

Bioshock Infinite and *Burial at Sea* ask us to think about what opening up gaming culture might actually entail. They dramatize the fear of creating stories that appeal to different demographics—the fear that they might end up killing off the types of stories that have been popular throughout history. But they also instill hope by offering examples of the kinds of compelling new stories and mechanics that could arise in their place, if they aren't smothered in their crib by an avalanche of new game releases featuring the same old story.

From #GamerGate to Donald Trump

TOXIC MASCULINITY AND THE POLITICS OF THE ALT-RIGHT

GAMERGATE, THE SOCIAL MEDIA—DRIVEN consumer hate campaign that has been going on in gaming culture since 2014, started as nothing more than a gossipy blog post from a jilted boyfriend bent on getting revenge on his ex. On August 16, 2014, Eron Gjoni, former paramour of indie game designer Zoë Quinn, wrote "The Zoe Post," a 9,000-odd-word screed detailing what he characterized as Quinn's abusive ways and her trysts with other gaming industry professionals and journalists. He even used screen caps of their private text messages and e-mails as evidence of her misdeeds.

Apparently this still wasn't enough punishment for Quinn, so Gjoni went one step further and began seeding links to "The Zoe Post" in gaming forums all over the Internet. It was later picked up by *4chan*, a notorious hub for trolls. Gjoni's goal: to call a swarm of Internet trolls down on his ex. Quinn later told a judge (during a hearing to get a restraining order against Gjoni), "Eron has coached this mob multiple times, made multiple social media accounts to smear my name publicly, and has stoked the fire of this on many occasions and doesn't seem to be stopping." In fact, according to Zachary Jason (2015),

> Gjoni worked overtime to make sure readers would keep coming back for more. Stoking the mob, he joined *4chan* discussion boards and released additional information online, including Quinn's supposed location and baseless theories on her sex life. Despite tacking a disclaimer onto his post—"I DO NOT STAND BY THE CURRENT ABUSE AND HARASSMENT OF ZOE QUINN OR FRIENDS. STOP DOING THAT. IT IS NOT IN ANYONE'S BEST INTEREST"—Gjoni taunted Quinn directly over Twitter and claimed online to be acting as a puppet master.

Indeed, as Quinn later proved in a screen cap fest of her own, Gjoni was participating in *4chan* "raid channels" (live chats used to plan and coordinate harassment) and on *Reddit* discussion boards in an effort to orchestrate the horde of trolls he had created (Social Justice Bread 2014).

But once the troops had been assembled and unleashed, they were unsatisfied with a single target. The scope of their mission began to expand from messing with Quinn, who happened to be an outspoken feminist, to messing with anyone involved in the gaming industry who professed an interest in social justice. The first target was the gaming news site *Kotaku*, which was accused of sheltering a journalist named Nathan Grayson. Grayson had supposedly published a positive review of Quinn's game *Depression Quest* in exchange for sexual favors from her. *Kotaku*'s editor in chief, Stephen Totilo (2014), dispelled these rumors by pointing out that "Nathan never reviewed Zoë Quinn's game *Depression Quest*, let alone gave it a favorable review." From these baseless allegations, however, the trolls were able to devise a cover story for their movement. They were actually for "ethics in gaming journalism" and against the politically correct "censorship" they thought feminist and antiracist pop culture critics were imposing on the medium via their biased reviews. This shift in focus made it easy to add more targets to the hit list, including Anita Sarkeesian (whose previous harassment over a video series she created to highlight problematic depictions of women in video games is described in more detail in Chapter 1), Leigh Alexander, Brianna Wu, and others.[1] As an analysis by *Newsweek* and BrandWatch of tweets using the #GamerGate hashtag during 2014 found, these targets were not chosen because of their journalistic sins—indeed, the targets for the most part were not journalists at all. For example, between game creator Zoë Quinn and games journalist Nathan Grayson, guess which one received the highest volume of negative tweets? "Twitter users have tweeted at Quinn using the #GamerGate hashtag 10,400 times since September 1. Grayson has received 732 tweets with the same hashtag during the same period. If GamerGate is about ethics among journalists, why is the female developer receiving 14 times as many outraged tweets as the male journalist?" (Wofford 2014). The same study found that Anita Sarkeesian and indie game developer Brianna Wu also received 35,188 and 38,952 tweets during the same period. In fact, "combined, these two women [got] more tweets on the #GamerGate hashtag than all the games journalists *Newsweek* looked at combined." In other words, the data show that "GamerGaters cares less about ethics and more about harassing women" (Wofford 2014).

However, it is important to ask where exactly this impulse to harass is coming from. It would be comforting to believe that gamers are some kind of uniquely barbaric and hateful subculture of basement dwellers and forty-year-old virgins who live in their mothers' basements. It is true that the rhetoric of the #GamerGate protest explicitly revolved around gaming tropes like "leveling up," "grinding" and "defeating the final boss" (Cross 2016b, 24–25). However, #GamerGate is just as much a product of mainstream gender politics as it is of video game culture. It is merely one of several reactionary outbursts arising out of the cultural backlash against feminism, antiracist activism, and gay rights activism; it is just one of several reactionary factions that essentially live online in a collection of blogs and forums, on *Reddit*, and in the bowels of *4chan*. And they are beginning to collaborate—offering each other fellowship, teaching each other their political vocabularies and talking points, providing each other with public relations advantages, and even mobilizing to support the campaigns of candidates like President Donald Trump.

Men's Rights Activism

THE ANTIFEMINIST BACKLASH ONLINE

Seeing as how most of the main targets of #GamerGate are feminist game designers and critics, it makes sense that some of the Internet's most vocal enemies of feminism, so-called men's rights activists, or MRAs, would use the hashtag-based movement as a recruitment opportunity. MRA groups are typically "made up of disenfranchised young men, father's rights advo-cates, male victims of domestic and sexual abuse, and members of the Pick Up Artist[2] movement" ("Men's Rights Movement" 2015). They may go by different names, such as the men's rights movement, the fathers' rights movement, or Men Going Their Own Way; they may focus on different top-ics; and they even squabble among themselves from time to time. However, what unites them is the nagging sense that everything that goes wrong in their lives is feminism's fault.

Susan Faludi has described the state of gender relations in the United States as one of "antifeminist backlash . . . set off not by women's achieve-ment of full equality but by the increased possibility that they might win it" (1991, 11). One of the signature myths of the backlash is the notion that the success of feminist projects means that men are now the ones getting a raw deal. As Roy Den Hollander, a men's rights movement lawyer who filed reverse discrimination lawsuits against bars that offered ladies' night promotions (Kimmel 2013, 373) and universities with women's and gender studies programs but no men's studies programs, put it, men were start-ing to believe that there were "now two classes of people in America: one of princesses—females, and the other of servants—males. Governments, from local to state to federal, treat men as second class citizens whose rights can be violated with impunity when it benefits females" (Kimmel 2013, 369). Out of this sense of frustration and fear came today's MRAs, whom Michael Kimmel describes as "a loose but loud collection of Inter-net blog sites, policy-oriented organizations, and legions of middle-class white men who feel badly done by individual women or by policies they believe have cheated them" (2013, 102). Their defining "core experience" is "aggrieved entitlement. It is that sense that those benefits to which you believed yourself entitled have been snatched away from you by unseen forces larger and more powerful" (18). They think that "men are the victims of reverse discrimination in every political, economic, and social arena" (102) and that "feminism has been so successful that men are now the sec-ond sex, and men have to stand up for their rights" (102).

While the idea of advocating for men's causes, including things like en-suring that male victims of rape and domestic abuse have access to help, is important and necessary, MRAs are seemingly more interested in making sure that women and feminists get their comeuppance than they are in actually helping men (Kelly 2013). For example, Paul Elam (aka "The Happy Misogynist"), founder of the flagship website dedicated to men's rights,

A Voice for Men, declared on his blog, "Should I be called to sit on a jury for a rape trial, I vow publicly to vote not guilty, even in the face of overwhelming evidence that the charges are true" (Serwer and Baker 2015). Pickup artist Roosh Valizadeh (2015), on the other hand, argues that the best way to eliminate rape is to legalize it when it takes place on private property:

> If rape becomes legal under my proposal, a girl will protect her body in the same manner that she protects her purse and smartphone. If rape becomes legal, a girl will not enter an impaired state of mind where she can't resist being dragged off to a bedroom with a man who she is unsure of—she'll scream, yell, or kick at his attempt while bystanders are still around. If rape becomes legal, she will never be unchaperoned with a man she doesn't want to sleep with. After several months of advertising this law throughout the land, rape would be virtually eliminated on the first day it is applied.

The Southern Poverty Law Center, an organization that monitors hate groups, calls the men's rights movement "misogynists" who "spread false claims about women" generally (Potok and Schlatter 2012) and who direct harassment and abuse at women online (Goldwag 2012). It makes sense, then, that MRAs would look at #GamerGate and see a group of kindred spirits. Several hot spots in the online "manosphere" laid out the welcome mat for #GamerGate. In October 2014, the "neomasclinist" website *Return of Kings* posted a job opening for a GamerGate correspondent that read, in part, "There is one important thing that ROK and GamerGate have in common: we have the same enemy. SJW's have plagued our corner of the sphere (often called the manosphere) for many years. . . . The enemy of my enemy is my friend" (Valizadeh 2014). Paul Elam of *A Voice for Men*, in a Twitter message, even offered to "bring soldiers" with him to the #GamerGate cause (@AVoiceForMen 2014).

Furthermore, MRAs have helped to shape the narrative #GamerGate presents to the wider world. According to this narrative, #GamerGate is a group of underdogs who were tired of being abused by feminists and other SJWs, and who banded together and stood up for themselves against the tyranny of political correctness. #GamerGate has taken up several memes and bits of terminology that are common in MRA circles to describe their so-called insurrection. Many #GamerGate-related tweets and blog posts mention "the red pill" or "red pilling." This phrase is a reference to the technopunk film *The Matrix* (1999) in which the main character, Neo, must choose between taking a red pill and learning the truth about the mysterious forces controlling his world, or taking a blue pill and remaining in ignorance and comfort. According to British newsmagazine *The Week*,

> *The Matrix* reference is often used by men's rights activists to identify each other in online forums. They use the term Red Pill as a metaphor for discovering that the world is an illusion and that men are slaves.
>
> "Until you know the red pill you exist in the world of shadows and lies," said one MRA. "You are a slave to the matriarchy. Break your chains, join the freedom-fighting men listening and seeing, and you will learn the truth and be free." ("Men's Rights Movement" 2015)

Another common MRA term that pops up in #GamerGate discourse is "virtue signaling." Virtue signaling is a performative act of self-righteousness that MRAs attribute to feminists and SJWs, whose overly earnest, emotional investment in their politics is labeled as uncool try-hard posturing (see Chapter 1). Virtue signaling is an ostentatious display of "the right, approved, liberal media-elite opinions" in a more-lefty-than-thou-style political correctness competition said to take place in social justice circles (Bartholomew 2015). To be fair, although there are many folks out there whose refusal to ever discuss anything other than politics and whose tendency to pat themselves on the back for their many enlightened views can be quite irritating, #GamerGate deploys the term to refer to anyone who expresses a political point of view to the left of Joe McCarthy. The assumption is that there are no sincere players in the social justice game. There are only the trolls who pretend to hold feminist and antiracist beliefs to show off how good they are, and the countertrolls who take pleasure in tweaking the noses of the fakers and exposing them as the frauds they are. Of course, this narrative is itself a subtle bit of trolling designed to goad ideological opponents into an unseemly display of emotion as they protest about how much they actually do care—or as David Shariatmadari (2016) put it, "The phrase ['virtue signaling'] serves two functions: to make your opponent look shallow, while at the same time (irony klaxon) signaling your initiation into a more sophisticated level of discourse."

Finally, any discourse designed to shore up a threatened masculinity is incomplete without some special gendered insults to describe those who don't follow the party line. In the MRA world, terms like "beta," "cuck" (for "cuckold") and "mangina" are used to describe those men who, in their minds, betray their gender by advocating for feminist positions. The word "cuck" also has a racial connotation, as it is often used to describe a weak white man whose woman is being stolen by an "alpha male" black man (Lewis 2015). This means that the word "cuck" appeals to the other major political group reaching out to #GamerGate: the white supremacist alternative right.

The Rise of the Alt-Right

MR. TROLL GOES TO WASHINGTON

To hear them tell it, the alt-right is a sort of second coming of the counter-cultural revolution of the 1960s, only moving in the opposite direction: a countercounterculture, if you will. Allum Bokhari and Milo Yiannopoulos (2016) at the conservative website *Breitbart* describe the movement as a "previously . . . obscure subculture" that "burst onto the national political scene in 2015," characterized by its "youthful energy and jarring, taboo-defying rhetoric that have boosted its membership and made it impossible to ignore." They identify several factions that contribute to the movement, including the aforementioned "online 'manosphere,' the nemeses of left-wing feminism," which "quickly became one of the alt-right's most distinctive constituencies," as well as "natural conservatives," the "mostly white, mostly male middle-American radicals, who are unapologetically embracing a new identity politics that prioritizes the interests of their own demographic." The natural conservatives share ties with white supremacists like Richard Spencer, the man who coined the term "alternative right" in the first place ("Alt Right: A Primer" 2016), and Jared Taylor, whose theory of race realism "co-opts evolutionary biology in the hopes of demonstrating that the races have become sufficiently differentiated over the millennia to the point that the races are fundamentally—that is, biologically—different" (Tuttle 2016).

Then there are the full-on neo-Nazis, the 1488ers who don't bother to dress up their racism in highfalutin philosophical or pseudo-scientific rhetoric. According to the Anti-Defamation League's website,

> 1488 is a combination of two popular white supremacist numeric symbols. The first symbol is 14, which is shorthand for the "14 Words" slo-

gan: "We must secure the existence of our people and a future for white children." The second is 88, which stands for "Heil Hitler" (H being the 8th letter of the alphabet). Together, the numbers form a general endorsement of white supremacy and its beliefs. As such, they are ubiquitous within the white supremacist movement—as graffiti, in graphics and tattoos, even in screen names and e-mail addresses, such as aryan-princess1488@hate.net. Some white supremacists will even price racist merchandise, such as t-shirts or compact discs, for $14.88.

If Bokhari and Yiannopoulos (2016) are to be believed, the 1488ers only come around because "anything associated as closely with racism and bigotry as the alternative right will inevitably attract real racists and bigots." That is, it's the mainstream media's fault that Nazi sympathizers are attaching themselves to the alt-right. Besides, Bokhari and Yiannopoulos (2016) argue, most in the alt-right movement "would rather the 1488ers didn't exist" at all: "Every ideology has them. Humourless ideologues who have no lives beyond their political crusade, and live for the destruction of the great. They can be found on *Stormfront* and other sites, not just joking about the race war, but eagerly planning it. They are known as 'Storm-fags' by the rest of the internet." Note that the way these self-appointed standard bearers for the alt-right movement choose to distance themselves from white supremacists is to question the masculinity of the 1488ers and insult their unseemly, overly emotional investment in their cause. "Joking about the race war" is posited as an acceptable practice because doing so implies an aloof, disdainful distance from the topic of racism in American society that is only possible from a position of privilege. Making pseudo-intellectual devil's advocate arguments about biological differences between the races is also apparently A-OK. But actually caring about questions of race, either as a SJW or as a white supremacist? That's faggy.

Meme-ifying Politics

So those are the origins of the alt-right: a loose collection of political Internet trolls that Rosie Gray (2015) accurately sums up as a mixture of "4chan-esque racist rhetoric combined with a tinge of Silicon Valley–flavored philosophizing, all riding on the coattails of the Trump boom." Indeed, the rise of Donald Trump has vaulted the alt-right into the public eye in an

unprecedented way. Trump's embrace of the alt-right, his willingness to repeat and retweet their memes and talking points on social media (Warzel
2016; Herrman 2016), and to enter one of their most popular *Reddit* hubs,
r/The_Donald, for an Ask Me Anything interview, has lent them an air of
political legitimacy they've never had in the past (Figure 8).

But where does #GamerGate fit in to all this? Why would a group who
professes to want to get politics out of video games hitch their wagon to
an explicitly political movement? From the moment that #GamerGate ap-
peared on Twitter's horizon, the racist wing of the alt-right saw a recruitment opportunity,[3] a way they could "insert their slogans—and ideas—into
the mainstream" and "find a wider audience for their views" (Mayo 2015).
Internet and pop culture–savvy #GamerGaters provided an ideal vehicle
for their digital Trojan horses. They would lend a frisson of youthful energy
and humor to old-fashioned racist, sexist, and homophobic politics.

As one white nationalist told Olivia Nuzzi (2016), "In a sense, we've
managed to push white nationalism into a very mainstream position . . .
Trump's online support has been crucial to his success, I believe, and the
fact is that his biggest and most devoted online supporters are white nationalists. Now, we've pushed the Overton window. People have adopted
our rhetoric, sometimes without even realizing it. We're setting up for a
massive cultural shift." Thus, #GamerGate (alongside *4chan* and certain
corners of *Reddit*) can be thought of as one arm of the alt-right's meme
team, the front men and women who translate old-fashioned fascism into
something that might be considered revolutionary and cool:

> Just as the kids of the 60s shocked their parents with promiscuity,
> long hair and rock'n'roll, so too do the alt-right's young meme brigades
> shock older generations with outrageous caricatures, from the Jewish
> "Shlomo Shekelburg" to "Remove Kebab," an internet in-joke about the
> Bosnian genocide. These caricatures are often spliced together with
> Millennial pop culture references, from old 4chan memes like Pepe the
> frog, to anime and *My Little Pony* references. . . .
>
> Young people perhaps aren't primarily attracted to the alt-right be-
> cause they're instinctively drawn to its ideology: they're drawn to it
> because it seems fresh, daring and funny, while the doctrines of their
> parents and grandparents seem unexciting, overly-controlling and
> overly-serious. (Bokhari and Yiannopoulos 2016)

Donald J. Trump ✓
@realDonaldTrump

Follow ∨

"@codyave: @drudgereport @BreitbartNews @Writeintrump "You Can't Stump the Trump" youtube.com/watch?v=MKH6PA... "

1:53 AM - 13 Oct 2015

8,546 Retweets **11,906** Likes

Figure 8. Donald Trump retweets a meme featuring the alt-right white supremacist icon Pepe the Frog. @realDonaldTrump, *Twitter*, October 13, 2015.

However, even as the men's rights movement and the alt-right were using #GamerGate as a recruitment tool, #GamerGate was teaching MRAs and the alt-right their extremely effective strategies for muddying the waters when the mainstream media accused them of racism and sexism: simply claim that anything seemingly too disgusting or extreme or offensive seen coming out of the movement is nothing more than the work of some un-affiliated trolls, not sincerely held beliefs of members of the movement meant to be taken seriously. Bokhari and Yiannopoulos (2016), for ex-ample, explain that for many of the troops in the alt-right's meme army, "their true motivations" are "lulz" and "not racism, the restoration of mon-archy or traditional gender roles." Their goal, they claim, is to "trigger the SJWers" for laughs (Singal 2016), to push back against political correctness and revel in absurdist free speech. In an online environment where caring deeply about issues and responding with emotion is considered uncool, the alt-right paints itself as the party of indifference, the apolitical party of the Internet age backing a presidential candidate whose primary draws are his Washington outsider status and his willingness to say just about anything to get media attention in the form of outrage.

Yet as I discuss in Chapter 3, pretending to be above politics is itself a political stance. #GamerGate and the alt-right may not really mean it when they threaten female journalists and game developers with rape and mur-der. They may not be truly passionate about harassing women and non-white people off the Internet. But their relentless attacks on anyone who cares about sexism and racism will inevitably bring about a similar result. Then, when all of their targets have headed for the hills, they will blame their victims for being "too sensitive" and "unable to take a joke." As Ken White told Rosie Gray (2015) in an interview, "It's really hard to tease out the genuine white nationalists from the trolls," but "at a certain point, the distinction isn't meaningful. If you spend all day saying white nationalist things online but you claim you're doing it ironically, it's not clear to me what the difference really is." As Katherine Cross (2016a) put it, "The per-formance of anti-Semitism has, in essence, *become* the new anti-Semitism; [4]channer sexism and racism, meanwhile, whether honest or not, still have the same impact as 'sincere' bigotry."

It makes sense that Donald Trump, the man who made a name for him-self in politics by vowing that he was "not a politician" (NewsThisSecond 2016), would be the candidate of #GamerGate. His followers' anxieties around immigration and fear of the changing racial demographics in the

United States are the fears of hardcore gamers worried about losing their privileges, only on a much larger scale. His apparent need to bolster his own masculinity by attacking women, calling them "fat," "ugly" ("Clinton's New Ad" 2016) "pigs," "dogs," and "slobs" (Farley 2015), is a signature move in the game of trolling.

Trump's success in capturing the Republican nomination and ultimately the presidency was a study in the power of trolling as a rhetorical strategy. In February 2014, long before Trump's presidential campaign began in earnest, McKay Coppins (2014) asked him about his contentious relationship with the media: "I ask Trump if he has ever heard the word 'trolling,' and at his request, I define it for him. He mulls it over for a second, and then confesses, 'I do love provoking people. There is truth to that. I love competition, and sometimes competition is provoking people. I don't mind provoking people. Especially when they're the right kind of people.'" Throughout the election season and in the early days of his administration, Trump used trollish tactics to get the best of his opponents, to throw them off of their usual game and get them responding to his antics instead of articulating their own positions. "That's why he calls every unflattering story about him 'fake news,' and why both he and his surrogates have repeatedly made reference to nonexistent attacks. It includes lying about crimes committed by immigrants and Chicago's murder rate, and about the number of people affected by his travel ban" (Cross 2017). Meanwhile, he himself would eschew things like policy details (too serious, too boring) and instead make speeches using repetitive, memelike structures and relying heavily on name calling (see Viser 2016). By baiting opponents into responding with emotion, Trump believes that he makes himself look bold and decisive and, as the election results ultimately showed, many voters agreed.

Trump truly is America's first ever troll president, but that doesn't mean that he should be dismissed or taken lightly. Rather, it means that he has mastered the art of harnessing supposedly unserious, insincere rhetoric toward serious (and I would argue dangerous) aims, an art that is the hallmark of Internet discourse. He has truly internalized the idea that politics is a game just begging to be hacked. And, as always, gamers have found themselves on the cutting edge, using their understanding of gamelike systems and online communication to develop devastatingly effective strategies. If the rest of us want to have a fighting chance, we are going to have to acknowledge that, like it or not, we are playing a game they already know well, and that they are willing to play dirty.

Epilogue: The Dating Game

GENDER PERFORMANCE AND GAMIFICATION IN THE REAL WORLD

ENDER IS AN IMPORTANT (if not the most important) factor in the social construction of gamer culture. But the question remains: what can gamer culture teach us about how gender operates IRL?[1] The logics of gaming are making their way into a variety of new contexts as marketers, business people, educators, activists, and politicians realize the strength of gaming as a rhetorical and motivational tool (Bogost 2012). Gamified concepts are even making their way into the world of love and romance as online dating and apps like Tinder become increasingly popular as a way to meet people. Some are even taking the gamificiation of the dating scene literally. Pickup artists, or PUAs, are groups of young men intent on "cracking the code that is woman" (Strauss 2007, 25). They want to take what they've learned about gender and sexuality in the virtual world and apply it to the real world. Made famous by Neil Strauss's best-selling 2005 memoir, exposé, and PUA guide *The Game*, PUAs can be found meeting up and comparing notes on their most recent "missions" (2007, 17) on various forums and message boards all over the web, including *PUA Forums*, *MPUA Forum*, and *The Attraction Forums*.

Pickup artistry is also a business, as websites such as *Real Social Dynamics*, *Venusian Arts*, and *PUA Artist* attest, in which charismatic entrepreneurs present a gamified version of gender relations to their clients. PUA experts promise their clients that by using their teachings like a sexual cheat code, they can have the women of their dreams. The goal of the PUA is to turn the subjective process of building attraction into an "algorithm" (Mystery 2007, 2) that they can refine to perfect their efficiency within the dating pool. Thus, they describe the lines and stories used on women as "routines" (Strauss 2007, 205) and "scripts" (211) (terms used by computer programmers) or "openers" (214) and "gambits" (Mystery 2007, 171) (terms used by chess players).

Strauss refers to pickup artistry as a "technology" (2005, 42) that guys can use to "short-circuit . . . the female brain" (2007, 211). Master PUA Mystery, aka Erik von Markovik, the subject of Strauss's book and the host of two seasons of the VH1 reality show *The Pickup Artist* (2007–8), notes that human beings are "beautiful, elegant biological machines embedded with sophisticated behavioral systems" (2007, 7) and brags that, using his system, his pupils will learn the process of "rewiring her attraction circuitry" (24).

The emphasis on converting the often fluid and amorphous world of social interaction into a quantifiable, transparent computer program makes sense when one considers the target demographic for pickup artistry: geeky guys who feel threatened by "alpha males" (Strauss 2005, 475). Alpha males are the confident, physically handsome, muscular men whom PUAs see as their most potent competition. Strauss, on the other hand, constantly refers to himself and his fellow PUAs as "nerds" (2005, 7, 42). Mystery confesses as much in his book: "If you're thinking, *Yeah, that worked for you, but it will never work for me; I'm a geek*, don't worry. I was a geek, too. The truth is, generally speaking, geeks are intelligent individuals who simply haven't yet applied that intelligence to social scenarios; hence they appear deficient in that area" (2007, 7). Yet the geek persona is also something that PUAs take pride in; even as they self-depreciatingly label themselves as socially awkward, they also brag that the intellectual strengths that they believe will allow them to outperform their more traditionally masculine counterparts. According to Strauss, who went by the PUA alias "Style," "Put [master PUAs] on South Beach in Miami and any number of better-looking, muscle-bound bullies will be kicking sand in their pale, emaciated faces. But put them in a Starbucks or Whisky Bar, and they'll be taking turns making out with that bully's girlfriend as soon as his back is turned" (2005, 12–13). In a dynamic similar to the ones discussed in earlier chapters, the women in this story are not in direct competition with the PUA. PUAs are in competition with their fellow men. The women are the objects of competition. They are the game pieces to be moved and the prizes to be won. Each of these guides makes the assumption that "players" are straight men, and that "scoring" (2005, 19), or accumulating sexual partners, is their victory condition. Women are also scored, but only in terms of their desirability to men: an average-looking woman rates as a 6 or a 7, while a beautiful model is a 9 or a 10 (2005, 96).

There are many indications in PUA literature that the pickup world is thought of as similar to a video game or a tabletop role-playing game. Like online gamers, PUAs go by aliases (Strauss 2005, 3), and they meet up in "lairs" (13) or in secret password-protected online communities where they trade notes on what works and what doesn't. Their lingo is full of acronyms and specialized jargon; instead of referring to BFGs[2] and KDAs[3], they speak of "AFCs" (475)—average frustrated chumps, who are unable to close the deal with the women they are attracted to—and "LMR" (480)—last-minute resistance, which must be overcome by the PUA once he and his target reach the bedroom. Much of their slang sounds like it comes straight out of *Halo: Combat Evolved* (Bungie, Microsoft Game Studios, 2001) or *Call of Duty*. They bandy about terms like "wing," "target," and "obstacle" (28), and Mystery (2007) often tells his students to think of their forays into night-clubs and bars "as if [they] were learning a new video game" (40): "If your man dies, just hit the reload button and play again" (42). One of his pupils took the metaphor one step further, breathlessly telling his fellow PUAs, "I'm into the game because it's like *Dungeons and Dragons*. When I learn a neg or a routine, it's like getting a new spell or a staff that I can't wait to use" (Strauss 2005, 89).

The gendered and sexualized logics of the gaming world have made their way into the world of pickup, and this has resulted in many of the same patterns of commodification and dehumanization of women appearing in PUA culture. Strauss seems to be intermittently aware of this fact, lamenting that he

> was beginning to see women solely as measuring instruments to give me feedback on how I was progressing as a pickup artist. They were my crash-test dummies, identifiable only by hair colors and numbers—a blonde 7, a brunette 10. Even when I was having a deep conversation,

learning about a woman's dreams and point of view, in my mind I was just ticking off a box in my routine marked rapport. In bonding with men, I was developing an unhealthy attitude toward the opposite sex. (2005, 96)

However, in his PUA lifestyle guide, *The Rules of the Game* (2007), he embraces this development, telling wannabe PUAs to think of women as nothing more than "walking sources of feedback" (112) in the great game of dating and mating being played among men.

PUA culture has even adopted the dominant discourse pattern of gaming culture: trolling. However, they have rebranded the troll into something they call the "neg": "Neither compliment nor insult, a neg is something in between—an accidental insult or backhanded compliment. The purpose of a neg is to lower a woman's self esteem while actively displaying a lack of interest in her—by telling her she has lipstick on her teeth, for example, or offering her a piece of gum after she speaks" (Strauss 2005, 23). Negs, much like troll posts, rely on plausible deniability to function. They are delivered to provoke an emotional reaction from the target but are designed to resemble gentle teasing jokes or inadvertent, mild insults, thus providing protection for the PUA if a target were to call him on his strategy. Examples of negs include comments like these:

> "Is that a wig? Oh . . . well it looks nice anyway."
> "I like that skirt. I just saw a girl wearing it a few minutes ago."
> "You kinda have man hands." (41)

And my absolute favorite neg:

> "Those shoes look really comfortable." (41)

Even outside of PUAdom, online dating is also home to many trolls. However, rather than using negging as a (purportedly) playful way to engage with a target, the trolls of online dating use tactics like threats and harassment to save face when they are rebuffed. They use trolling as a discursive means to reassert control over a situation in which a woman has expressed the desire to cut off contact. Expressing interest in a woman online means that men must doff the mask of cool aloofness that protects them.

When faced with rejection, they retreat back behind that mask, claiming to have only messaged the target "for the lulz" in the first place.

Alexandra Tweten, the creator of the Tumblr *Bye Felipe*, chronicles the exploits of this type of troll. Tweten (2014) notes that "it has become apparent that a standard trajectory of discourse with men online is this: Man hits on woman, woman rejects or ignores him, man lashes out with insults or even threats." "They're trying to make us feel bad about making them feel bad," she told the *Atlantic*. "They're just trying to strike at whatever our insecurities are. You were just interested a second ago, and now you're saying, you have a fat ugly nose" (Khazan 2014). *Bye Felipe* and several websites like it, including *Straight White Boys Texting* and *Reddit's Creepy PMs*, function as gendered hacks of the discursive field around online dating. Their creators use their knowledge of the web and their familiarity with the codes of trollspeak to counter the rhetorical onslaughts women face online, revealing the patterns in online harassment and draining barbs of their sting even as they publicly shame harassers.

Furthermore, such archives are educational tools; they can serve as proof that being a woman online is tough. One *Reddit* user discovered as much for himself when he decided to perform an experiment to prove that "girls have it easy on dating sites" (OKCThrowaway22221 2014) because they can pick and choose from among hundreds or even thousands of men who would be happy to get a date with anybody. When he started to receive messages from guys before he could even finish filling out a female profile, he thought he had proven his hypothesis. But then,

> as more and more messages came (either replies or new ones I had about 10 different guys message me within 2 hours) the nature of them continued to get more and more irritating. Guys were full-on spamming my inbox with multiple messages before I could reply to even one asking why I wasn't responding and what was wrong. Guys would become hostile when I told them I wasn't interested in NSA sex, or guys that had started normal and nice quickly turned the conversation into something explicitly sexual in nature. Seemingly nice dudes in quite esteemed careers asking to hook up in 24 hours and sending [sic] them naked pics of myself despite multiple times telling them that I didn't want to.
>
> I would be lying if I said it didn't get to me. I thought it would be some fun thing, something where I would do it and worse [sic] case scenario

say "lol I was a guy I trolle you lulz" etc. but within a 2 hour span it got me really down and I was feeling really uncomfortable with everything.

He concludes, "I came away thinking that women have it so much harder than guys do when it comes to that kind of stuff."

Hackers and pranksters also use online dating as their medium. Take as an example the case of a computer engineer going by the name of Patrick who created gender trouble and "pitted heterosexual male against heterosexual male" using Tinder:

Patrick's program identifies two men who "like" one of his bait profiles (the first used prominent vlogger Boxxy's image; the second used an acquaintance who had given Patrick consent) and matched them to each other. The suitors' messages—some aggressive, others mundane, but all of them unabashedly flirtatious—are then relayed, back and forth, to one another through the dummy profile.

Patrick was a Tinder user (in fact, it's where he met his current girl-friend) and says that female friends of his would often complain about the messages they received on Tinder. "The original idea was to throw that back into the face of the people doing it to see how they would react." (Zelenko 2015)

More importantly, an awareness of the way that gamelike structure is being imposed on interactions like dating can also be harnessed toward creating technological solutions that enable women to turn the tables in their favor. For example, the creators of Tinder, which was released in 2012 by Hatch Labs (Brown 2013), developed an interface that resembles a casual mobile game (Ganner 2014). It turns user profiles into playing cards that can be manipulated by simple, intuitive controls: swipe right if you like someone, or swipe left to skip over the candidate. Unlike other dating apps that require a large up-front investment of time and attention, Tinder lets users jump into the mix right away, swiping in short bursts when they have time. Users are even prompted by the interface to think of time spent swiping as playing:

Users have their own vocabulary: people don't "sign up" or "go on," they "play" Tinder. The randomized Matches and swipe-left-or-swipe-right physicality of the interface makes it feel more like a video game

than a life pursuit, and you can knock out a few rounds while waiting in line at the grocery store. It's so easy to pull out your phone,
pass it around a crowded bar table and come up with drinking games
for people you see (a shot for every guy who quotes *Fight Club*; finish
your beer for every profile whose lead photo features a more-attractive
friend in the shot). (Brown 2013)

This game takes into account the gendered disparities in the experience
that Tinder users will have with online dating. Both members of a pairing
must swipe right on each other in order for them to be able to chat directly.
Men are thus unable to initiate contact with women unless the women
have indicated their willingness to chat first (and vice versa). This provides
a layer of protection for female users and solves one of the major problems
that plague online services: women become a scarce resource because they
are driven out by harassers and trolls. As one can imagine, such a development can spell doom for a dating service. Thus, it is in Tinder's best economic interest to create an app that will provide a greater level of safety
and comfort for female users specifically.

The marketing campaign for the premium version of the app, Tinder
Plus, demonstrates that women's experiences are important to developers.
Their website features a video in which a young woman reminisces about
her recent trip abroad. She meets one guy in London without the help of
the app and he turns out to be a disaster, abandoning her to get arrested
after a wild night. However, the guy she meets in Paris with the help of
the app is a keeper; he is depicted as sweet and thoughtful, and he even
surprises her by showing up with flowers at another stop along her trip.
The subtext of the ad suggests to women that Tinder is a product that will
help women to find adventure in relative safety. It will provide a means to
screen out troublemakers and provides a shortcut to quality hookups that
could possibly blossom into something more. This suggests that the app's
producers have actually thought through the problems (and dangers) that
women face when it comes to dating, romance, and hookups, and that they
developed their software specifically to help defuse those problems.

What is notable about services like Tinder (and similar apps like Anti-
date and Bumble, which also require women to opt in before chat is en-
abled) is that they model a new way of thinking about usability and ac-
cessibility when it comes to tech, one rooted in cultural paradigms. These
developers recognized a specific need that gender-neutral dating apps (that

is, apps that failed to take into account the disparities between the experiences that men and women were having on the platform) were unable to meet. They then reasoned that there was a profit to be made in building in features aimed directly at making the platform a more welcoming place for women (see Condis 2015 for more).

Of course, PUAs are hard at work trying to figure out how to hack online dating systems like Tinder, including providing Tinder advice on *PUAmore* as well on as websites like *Tinder Seduction* and *Tinder Code*. It remains imperative for developers to consider the ever-evolving needs of women (and queer folk and people of color and the disabled and the poor and the elderly and any other demographic group that has gone unrecognized as a source of valuable participants in Internet culture) and to think about how the infrastructure of their communities can be exploited by trolls. Their willingness to do so will be tied to our willingness as consumers to convince them that it is worth their time and money to invest in making the web a more diverse place. Gaming mechanics and social hacks can solve many of these problems, but only if we create a financial incentive for developers so that they are willing to play alongside us.

NOTES

INTRODUCTION

1. For more on gamification as a tool used by corporations for marketing and employee training, see Werbach (2012), Bogost (2012), and Stanfill and Condis (2014). For more on gamification in education, see Gee (2007), Kapp (2012), Squire (2011), and Sheldon (2012). For gamification in politics and activism, see Galloway (2006). For the gamification of the labor of fans, see Stanfill and Condis (2014).

2. MUDs and MOOs are text-based chat room–esque virtual worlds that were common in the early days of the Internet. MUD stands for multiuser dungeon (or, later, multiuser domain), and MOO stands for "MUD, object oriented" (or a MUD with a persistent object database) (Rae 2001).

3. Porting refers to the process of converting software so that it can run on a different machine from the one it was initially designed to be used on.

BRO'S LAW

1. This posture has elsewhere been called "hipster sexism," "the idea that, because we all know that what we are seeing is sexism, we are in on the joke—which supposedly negates the sexism" (Murphy 2013). See also Quart (2012).

CHAPTER 1

1. Newbs (sometimes spelled "noobs" or "nubs") is short for "newbies," a derogatory term for inexperience or unskilled players.

2. Statistically, women and female-presenting users are much more likely to face trolling than are men and male-presenting users. According to the website of the nonprofit research group Working to Halt Online Abuse, between 2000 and 2008, 72.5 percent of those who reported experiencing on-

line harassment identified themselves as female while online; only 22 percent identified themselves as male. Likewise, Meyer and Cukier's (2006, 467)
study at the University of Maryland found that accounts with feminine user-
names Chat Client IRC received an average of 100 troll messages a day, while
masculine-sounding names only got an average of 3.7.

3. This last is a tendency that can be traced back to some of the earliest examples of online role-playing, as Julian Dibbell ([1998] 2015) pointed out in
"A Rape in Cyberspace," in which he recounts a case of how one virtual community chose to deal with an outbreak of textually constructed sexual assaults.

4. On the About page of its website, IGN Entertainment describes itself as
"a leading online media & services company obsessed with gaming, entertainment and everything guys enjoy." It is thus perhaps unsurprising that their
reality show competition was not very attentive to the difficulties experienced
by women in male-dominated spaces, like the fighting game community or
video game culture in general.

5. This practice is not unlike the hazing practices described by Hank Nuwer
(2004) as the initiation rites for sports teams, sororities, and fraternities.

6. Although *Penny Arcade* did eventually pull the shirts from their store,
saying that they didn't want to make anyone feel unwelcome at PAX (Krahulik
2011), Krahulik reignited the controversy in an interview with *Penny Arcade*
business manager Robert Khoo when he stated that "pulling the dickwolves
merchandise was a mistake" (Hernandez 2013).

7. Google bombing refers to the practice of creating numerous links re-
lating to a particular keyword in order to drive Google results of a search for
that word to a particular location. Often Google bombing is used to drive
searches toward embarrassing or satirical results.

8. "A distributed denial-of-service (DDoS) attack is one in which a multitude of compromised systems attack a single target, thereby causing denial of
service for users of the targeted system. The flood of incoming messages to
the target system essentially forces it to shut down, thereby denying service to
the system to legitimate users" (Distributed Denial-of-Service Attack" 2013).
Another target of such tactics was the *Gamers Against Bigotry* website, which
was hacked to display racist slurs and graphic sexual images on its front page.
Hackers also wiped the site's database of pledges collected from gamers who
promised "to not use bigoted language while gaming, online and otherwise"
(Lewis 2012a).

9. Like trolling, hacking can be thought of as a textual performance of a
"Wild West brand of masculinity" (Adam 2003). As Adam (2003) notes, in
many popular accounts, the hacker is imagined as a modern-day cowboy, a
rugged individual penetrating a digital space and asserting control over it,

reshaping it by a combination of intelligence, technological superiority, and force of will. Hacking is thus culturally positioned as an enactment of masculinity that is well suited to the digital age.

10. One commentator amusingly phrased this sentiment in reference to Anita Sarkeesian: "If I slather myself with honey and put fish in my pockets and start pushing at bears, I don't really have a case when suddenly I get mauled. . . . When you go on the Internet with an opinion you are going to get backlash" ("No right answer," 2014). Note that this metaphor posits trolls as a mindless force of nature and not as a group of conscious individuals making the active decision to harass and threaten another person.

FAR CRY 3

1. For more on the racist, colonialist tropes in Conrad's *Heart of Darkness*, see Achebe (1977).

2. For an interesting take on the historical roots of *Far Cry 3*'s tattooing mechanic as a trope straight out of "the racist narratives of the Victorian freakshow," see Rath (2013).

3. See my Game Break on Bro's Law; and Payne (2016).

4. See Nakamura's (2002) discussion of virtual tourism.

CHAPTER 2

1. This is a device that allows gamers to cheat at console games by, for example, giving them extra lives or allowing players to become invulnerable or invisible.

2. Capitalization and grammar of the original posts are retained here.

3. According to research conducted by Yee (2005), who performs a detailed breakdown of player demographics, the most popular character class among women in *World of Warcraft* is the Hunter (24 percent of female players, damage-dealer class), followed by the Priest (19 percent of female players, healer class) and the Druid (14 percent of female players, utility class, which can transform into various animals, enabling players to take on different roles including dealing physical or magic damage, healing and buffing statistics, or soaking up enemy damage, also known as tanking).

4. This is the stereotype parodied by the *Twitch.tv* performer Kaceytron. See my Game Break on Bro's Law.

5. We might extrapolate from Edidin's (n.d.) countermeme manifesto the idea that gender itself, the hierarchical power structure created to define and differentially treat bodies, is itself a meme and that the ill treatment of women in gaming culture is merely one of the newer subgenres within that broader memeplex.

HACKS AND MODS

1. Lara Croft is a complex figure worthy of analysis far beyond what I can render here. She is a physically powerful and capable heroine, one of the few strong, recognizable female protagonists in gaming. She is also a famous pinup girl, a marketing figure designed to attract the male gaze. This makes the intense focus that hackers and modders have placed on Lara especially important, as they seemingly recognize her dual position as a feminist ambassador for gaming culture and an object for straight male gamers to play with. For more, see MacCallum-Stewart (2014) and Kennedy (2002).

2. Machinima is "digital performance that controls procedurally animated moving images" (Nitsche 2011, 121)—that is, animated movies that are recorded from within a digital world.

3. These kinds of mods function similarly to genres of fan fiction like slash, which is named for the / symbol that simultaneously combines and divides the names of two characters. Slash was created by women and queer readers as a means to imagine romantic or erotic encounters between same-sex characters (Salmon and Symons 2003). See also Wirman (2014).

4. For more on the history of gender-bending classic video game mods, see Weil (2013).

CHAPTER 3

1. It looks as though for a certain demographic of young men living in what Michael Kimmel calls Guyland that there is an entire "stage of life, a liminal undefined time span between adolescence and adulthood" (2008, 4) that has been explicitly set aside for play. Guyland is "a place, or, rather, a bunch of places where guys gather to be guys with each other, unhassled by the demands of parents, girlfriends, jobs, kids, and the other nuisances of adult life. In this topsy-turvy Peter-Pan mindset, young men shirk the responsibilities of adulthood and remain fixated on the trappings of boyhood" (5). Video games are a popular pastime for the residents of Guyland because they represent a way to avoid "the burdens of adult masculinity" (147), including forming relationships, getting started in their careers, and engaging with political issues. According to Kimmel, the fantasy world of media is both an escape from and to reality—the "'reality' that many of these guys secretly would like to inhabit. Video games, in particular, provide a way for guys to feel empowered. . . . It's a fantasy world of Manichean good and evil, a world in which violence is restorative, and actions have no consequences whatsoever" (150). At least, that is the argument coming from Guyland.

2. In the interest of recreating the rhetorical environment of the forums as accurately as possible, no attempt was made to clean up spelling or grammar

errors in posts made by gamers. However, some quotations have been short-ened so as to focus exclusively on the portions that are relevant to this study. Ellipses indicate removal of irrelevant or repetitive content.

3. During the peer review process for the publication of a version of this chapter in the journal *Convergence*, one anonymous referee noted that the technoutopian core of the Star Wars film franchise itself is also relevant to these fan-made arguments. After all, one of Yoda's greatest lessons for Luke about the ways of the Force is that the body of a Jedi is irrelevant. Only the mind and the spirit matter to the Jedi. As Master Yoda puts it in *The Empire Strikes Back* (1980), "Luminous beings are we, not this crude matter." How-ever, the introduction of midichlorians in *The Phantom Menace* (1999) as the source of the Force's power in the prequel films reverses this logic by rooting the Force in the body once more, a development roundly disdained by Star Wars fans. See Anders (2010).

4. For more on Bastal's "straight male gamer" rant, see Holmes (2016).

5. Bastal explicitly claims to be a "straight male gamer" in his post. I thus refer to him as male because this is the self-image he chooses to project on the thread.

CHAPTER 4

1. For an overview of #GamerGate history, see Hathaway (2014), Wagner (2014), and Kain (2014).

2. For more on pickup artistry, see the Epilogue.

3. Black hat hacker and white supremacist Andrew Auernheimer (Hate-watch Staff 2016), who goes by the nickname Weev, described #GamerGate as "by far the single biggest siren bringing people into the folds of white nation-alism" (Futrelle 2015).

EPILOGUE

1. "IRL" stands for "in real life," which typically refers to the physical world, as opposed to the virtual worlds constructed in games and online forums. However, the line between real and virtual is actually murky. Virtual pro-cesses and identities are increasingly coming to inform our real-world identi-ties, and the logic of gamification is taking over many real-world relationships and interactions. See also Lehdonvirta (2010).

2. In classic first-person shooters like *Doom* (id Software, GT Interactive, 1993) and *Quake* (id Software, GT Interactive, 1996), BFG stands for "big fuck-ing gun."

3. In massive online battle arena–style games like *League of Legends* and *Defense of the Ancients 2* (Valve Corporation, 2013), KDA is the ratio of kills, deaths, and assists that a player racks up over the course of a game.

WORKS CITED

Achebe, Chinua. 1977. "An Image of Africa: Racism in Conrad's *Heart of Darkness*." *Massachusetts Review* 18:782–94.

Adam, A. E. 2003. "Hacking into Hacking: Gender and the Hacker Phenomenon." *ACM SIGCAS Computers and Society* 33 (4): 3.

Adam, Alison. 2002. "The Ethical Dimension of Cyberfeminism." In *Reload: Rethinking Women + Cyberculture*, edited by Mary Flanagan and Austin Booth, 158–74. Cambridge, MA: MIT Press.

Aikin, Scott F. 2013. "Poe's Law, Group Polarization, and Argumentative Failure in Religious and Political Discourse." *Social Semiotics* 23 (3): 301–17.

Aldred, Jessica, and Brian Greenspan. 2011. "A Man Chooses, a Slave Obeys: *BioShock* and the Dystopian Logic of Convergence." *Games and Culture* 6 (5): 479–96.

Alexander, Leigh. 2014. "'Gamers' Don't Have to Be Your Audience. 'Gamers' Are Over." *Gamasutra*, August 28.

"All the World's a Game." 2011. *Economist*, December 10.

Althusser, Louis. 1972. "Ideology and Ideological State Apparatuses." *Lenin and Philosophy and Other Essays*. New York: Monthly Review Press, 127–86.

"Alt Right: A Primer about the New White Supremacy." 2016. *Anti-Defamation League*, October 19.

amanda b. 2013. "Filthy Casuals." *Know Your Meme*, May 9.

Anders, Charlie Jane. 2010. "The *Real* Problem with Midichlorians." *io9*, February 26.

"Announcing 1998 Mode." 2014. *Irrational Games Insider*, February 27.

Arendt, Susan. 2014. "Same sex marriage in Harvest Moon: 'We know what the fans are looking for.'" *Engadget*, June 13.

Atkins. 2014. "Why are resto druids and healing priests always girls?" *World of Warcraft Forums*, January 5.

@AVoiceforMen. 2014. "I am following and supporting anyone I see bearing #OpSKYNET #GamerGate #NotYourShield and I am bringing soldiers with me." *Twitter*, 17 November.

Barlow, John Perry. 1996. "A Declaration of the Independence of Cyberspace." *Electronic Frontier Foundation*.

Bartholomew, James. 2015. "The Awful Rise of 'Virtue Signalling.'" *Spectator*, April 18.

Bastal. 2011. "BioWare neglected their core audience: the straight male gamer" (message 1). *BioWare Social Network*.

Bernstein, Jospeh. n.d. "The *Kill Screen* Review: *Far Cry 3*, the First Game about the Millennials." *Kill Screen*.

Bertozzi, Elena. 2008. "'You play like a girl!': Cross-Gender Competition and the Uneven Playing Field. *Convergence* 14 (4): 473–88.

Birnbaum, Ian. 2013. "*World of Warcraft* Lost More than a Million Subscribers Last Quarter, Is Still Bigger than Everything Ever." *PC Gamer*, May 9.

Bishop, Jonathan. 2012. "Scope and Limitations in the Government of Wales Act 2006 for Tackling Internet Abuses in the Form of 'Flame Trolling.'" *Statute Law Review* 33 (2): 207–16.

Blackmore, Susan. 1999. *The Meme Machine*. Oxford: Oxford University Press.

Blake, Mariah. 2015. "Mad Men: Inside the Men's Rights Movement—And the Army of Misogynists and Trolls It Spawned." *Mother Jones* (January/February).

Bogost, Ian. 2007. *Persuasive Games: The Expressive Power of Videogames*. Cambridge, MA: MIT Press.

———. 2012. *How to Do Things with Video Games*. Minneapolis: University of Minnesota Press.

Bokhari, Allum, and Milo Yiannopoulos. 2016. "An Establishment Conservative's Guide to the Alt-Right." *Breitbart*, March 29.

Bolton, Doug. 2015. "Female Link, 'Linkle,' Introduced by Nintendo for Upcoming Zelda Game." *Independent*, November 13.

Bordo, Susan. 2003. *Unbearable Weight: Feminism, Western Culture, and the Body*. 10th anniversary ed. Berkeley: University of California Press.

Boyes, Emma. 2007. "EA: Women 'Too Big an Audience to Ignore.'" *Gamespot*, April 19.

Brabham, Daren C. 2014. "Crowdsourcing as a Model for Problem Solving: An Introduction and Cases." *Convergence* 20 (3): 75–90.

Brightman, James. 2006. "Women Gamers Outnumber Men?" *Bloomberg Business Week: Innovation and Design*, April 18.

Brown, August. 2013. "Perfect Strangers: Tinder and 21st Century Fiction." *Los Angeles Times Review of Books*, December 24.

Brown, Tara Tiger. 2012. "Dear Fake Geek Girls: Please Go Away." *Forbes*, March 26.

Burrill, Derek A. 2008. *Die Tryin': Videogames, Masculinity, Culture*. New York: Peter Lang.

Butler, Judith. 2007. *Gender Trouble: Feminism and the Subversion of Identity*. 2nd ed. New York: Routledge.

Cambria, Erik, Praphul Chandra, Avinash Sharma, and Amir Hussain. 2010. "Do Not Feel the Trolls." In *Proceedings of the 3rd International Workshop on Social Data on the Web* (Shanghai, China). SDoW.

"Case Study: Changing the Game—Lessons from Nintendo's Wii." 2013. *MaRS*, May 22.

Citron, Danielle Keats. 2009. "Law's Expressive Value in Combating Cyber Gender Harassment." *Michigan Law Review* 108 (3): 373–415.

"Clinton's New Ad Reminds You of the Awful Things Trump Has Said about Women." 2016. *Sydney Morning Herald*, September 26.

Cole, Justin J. 2009. "The Impact of Homophobia in Virtual Communities." *Kotaku*, July 10.

Concelmo, Chad. 2010. "Brown Hair and Stubble: The New Face of Modern Videogames." *Destructoid*, July 15.

Condis, Megan. 2015. "The Game of Trolls and How to Win It." *Al Jazeera America*, March 28.

Cook, David. 2013. "Analyst: Games Costing $100 Million Need 5–10 Million Sales to Succeed." *VG 24/7*, March 27.

Coppins, McKay. 2014. "36 Hours on the Fake Campaign Trail with Donald Trump." *BuzzFeed*, February 13.

Cross, Katherine. 2016a. "How Online Harassment Is Setting the Tone for the 2016 Election." *Establishment*, May 26.

———. 2016b. "Press F to Revolt: On the Gamification of Online Activism." In *Diversifying Barbie and "Mortal Kombat": Intersectional Perspectives and Inclusive Designs in Gaming*, edited by Yasmin B. Kafai, Gabriela T. Richard, and Brendesha M. Tynes, 23–34. Pittsburgh, PA: ETC Press.

———. 2017. "How Trump Is Trying to Govern America Like an Internet Troll." *Rolling Stone*, February 23.

crossassaultharass. 2012. "Day 1: Sexual Harassment on *Cross Assault*" (video). *YouTube*, February 28.

Dawkins, Richard. 2006. *The Selfish Gene*. 30th anniversary ed. Oxford: Oxford University Press.

Denson, Shane. 2013. "Afterword: Framing, Unframing, Reframing: Retconning the Transnational Work of Comics." In *Transnational Perspectives on*

Graphic Novels: Comics at the Crossroads, edited by Shane Denson, Christina Meyer, and Daniel Stein, 271–84. London: Bloomsbury Academic.

Dibbell, Julian. (1998) 2015. "A Rape in Cyberspace. or TINYSOCIETY, and How to Make One." *Julian Dibbell*.

"Distributed Denial-of-Service Attack (DDoS)." 2013. *Search Security* (May).

Donath, Judith A. 1998. "Identity and Deception in the Virtual Community." In *Communities in Cyberspace*, edited by Peter Kollock and Marc A. Smith, 29–59. London: Routledge.

Dyer, Richard. 1997. *White*. London: Routledge.

Edidin, Rachel. 2012. "Who Are You to Say She's Not?" *Postcards from Space*, August 22.

Eisenberg, Rebecca L. 1998. "Girl Games: Adventures in Lip Gloss." *Gamasutra*, February 13.

Elikal. 2009. "GLBT discrimination in forums? Message 1. *Star Wars: The Old Republic Community*.

"Every Gaming System Has Its Fans, but Women Like Wii." 2009. *Nielsen Newswire*, February 17.

Faludi, Susan. 1991. *Backlash: The Undeclared War against American Women*. New York: Crown.

Farley, Robert. 2015. "Fact Check: Trump's Comments on Women." *USA Today*, August 12.

Fdzzaigl. 2009. "GLBT discrimination in forums?" (message 12). *Star Wars: The Old Republic Community*.

fimontronia. 2014. "Kaceytron truth. It's fraudulent." *Reddit*, August 20.

Flanagan, Mary. 2009. *Critical Play: Radical Game Design*. Cambridge, MA: MIT Press.

Foucault, Michel. 1990. *The History of Sexuality, Volume 1: An Introduction*. Translated by Robert Hurley. New York: Vintage.

Futrelle, David. 2015. "Weev: Gamergate Is 'The Biggest Siren Bringing People into the Folds of White Nationalism.'" *We Hunted the Mammoth*, August 24.

Gaider, David. 2011. "To the OP . . . " *BioWare Social Network*.

Galloway, Alexander R. 2006. *Gaming: Essays on Algorithmic Culture*. Minneapolis: University of Minnesota Press.

"Game Player Data." 2013. *Entertainment Software Association*, May 22.

gamespot. 2013. "Killer Instinct Smart Glass Demo E3 2013 MS Press Conference" (video). *YouTube*, June 10.

Ganner, Liz. 2014. "For Mobile Apps Like Tinder, Cards and Swipes Rule the Day." *Recode*, March 14.

Gaudiosi, John. 2013. "How Riot Games Created the Most Popular Game in the World." *CNN Money*, July 10.

Gee, James Paul. 2007. *What Video Games Have to Teach Us about Learning and Literacy*. Rev. and updated ed. New York: Palgrave Macmillan.

Gilbert, Ben. 2009. "Microsoft Talks to GLAAD about GLBT Policy Issues." *Joystiq*, April 14.

Gjoni, Eron. 2014. *thezoepost*.

"GLBT discrimination in forums?" 2009. *Star Wars: The Old Republic Community*.

Glockass. 2013. "Why Do Girls Always Play Healer Priests or Paladins? *GameFAQs*, May 2.

Goldfarb, Andrew. 2012. "Capcom and IGN Present *Cross Assault*." *IGN*, February 21.

Golding, Dan. 2014. "The End of Gamers." *Tumblr*, August 28.

Goldwag, Arthur. 2012. "Leader's Suicide Brings Attention to Men's Rights Movement." *Southern Poverty Law Center*, March 1.

Good, Owen. 2012. "Family Research Council: 'Rebel Fleet Surrenders to Gay Empire.'" *Kotaku*, January 28.

———. 2013. "She Hacked *The Legend of Zelda* So Now It Stars Zelda, Saving Link." *Kotaku*, March 16.

Gray, Rosie. 2015. "How 2015 Fueled the Rise of the Freewheeling, White Nationalist Alt-Movement." *BuzzFeed*, December 27.

Greenfield, Rebecca. 2013. "The Rape 'Joke' at Microsoft's E3 Reveal Is a Bigger Deal than Another Bad 'Joke.'" *Atlantic Wire*, June 10.

Gregar. 2014. Comment on "*BioShock Infinite* box art revealed." *Reddit*, December 1.

Griffiths, Daniel Nye. 2012a. "'Fake Geek Girls': How Geek Gatekeeping Is Bad for Business." *Forbes*, July 26.

———. 2012b. "'Girlfriend Mode,' *Borderlands 2*, and Why Being a Dude Rocks." *Forbes*, August 13.

Hamilton, Kirk. 2012. "The Fake Threat of Fake Geek Girls." *Kotaku*, March 27.

Hamilton, Mary. 2013. "*Star Wars: The Old Republic*, the Gay Planet, and the Problem of the Straight Male Gaze." *Guardian*, January 25.

Hardaker, Claire. 2010. "Trolling in Asynchronous Computer-Mediated Communication: From User Discussions to Academic Definitions." *Journal of Politeness Research* 6:215–42.

Hatewatch Staff. 2016. "Notorious Neo-Nazi Hacker and White Supremacist Website May Face Fines for Anti-Semitic Trolling." *Southern Poverty Law Center*, April 7.

Hathaway, Jay. 2014. "What Is Gamergate, and Why? An Explainer for Non-Geeks." *Gawker*, October 10.

Hernandez, Patricia. 2012a. "Here Are Three Possible Reasons for Including Rape in *Far Cry 3*." *Kotaku*, December 13.

———. 2012b. "Three Words I Said to the Man I Defeated in *Gears of War* That I'll Never Say Again." *Kotaku*, May 30.

———. 2013. "*Penny Arcade* Artist: Pulling Dickwolves Merchandise 'Was a Mistake.'" *Kotaku*, September 3.

———. 2014a. "*GTA Online* Mods Let People 'Rape' Other Players." *Kotaku*, August 8.

———. 2014b. "The Steam Achievement that Nobody Unlocked." *Kotaku*, July 28.

———. 2015. "The People Who Make Brutal Video Game Porn." *Kotaku*, March 11.

———. 2016a. "Inside the NSFW World of *Fallout* and *Skyrim* Nudity Mods." *Kotaku*, January 11.

———. 2016b. "The *Skyrim* Porn that Has Millions of Views on Pornhub." *Kotaku*, February 2.

Herring, Susan, Kirk Job-Sluder, Rebecca Scheckler, and Sasha Barab. 2002. "Searching for Safety Online: Managing 'Trolling' in a Feminist Forum." *Information Society* 18:371–84.

Herrman, John. 2016. "Donald Trump Finds Support in Reddit's Unruly Corners." *New York Times*, April 11.

Hinkley, Alexander. 2012. "New *BioShock Infinite* Box Art Causes Controversy." *Examiner*, December 3.

Holkins, Jerry, and Mike Krahulik. 2010a. "Breaking It Down." Web comic. *Penny Arcade*, August 13.

———. 2010b. "Simulacra." Web comic. *Penny Arcade*, August 29.

———. 2010c. "The Sixth Slave." Web comic. *Penny Arcade*, August 11.

Holmes, Steven. 2016. "Playing Past the 'Straight Male Gamer': From Modding Edwin(a) to Bisexual Zevran in *BioWare* Games." In *Gender and Sexuality in Contemporary Popular Fantasy: Beyond Boy Wizards and Kick-Ass Chicks*, edited by Jude Roberts and Esther MacCallum-Stewart, 117–32. New York: Routledge.

Huizinga, Johan. 1955. *Homo Ludens: A Study of the Play Element in Culture*. Boston: Beacon.

Husted, Kristofor. 2011. "Gamers Solve Stubborn Viral Mystery: The Shape of a Key Enzyme." *NPR*, September 19.

Hyman, Paul. 2007. "Casual Games: Too Much of a Good Thing?" *Bloomberg Business Week: Innovation and Design*, August 24.

indelible. 2009. "GLBT discrimination in forums?" (message 152). *Star Wars: The Old Republic Community*.

iplaywinner. 2012. *"Cross Assault*—Day 5—BBS HQ" (video). *Twitch.tv*, Feb-rurary 26.

Jason, Zachary. 2015. "Game of Fear." *Boston Magazine* (May).

Jenkins, Henry. 1992. *Textual Poachers: Television, Fans, and Participatory Culture.* New York: Routledge.

———. 2006. *Convergence Culture: Where Old and New Media Collide.* New York: New York University Press.

Jenkins, Henry, Sam Ford, and Joshua Green. 2013. *Spreadable Media: Creating Value and Meaning in a Networked Culture.* New York: New York University Press.

Johnston, Casey. 2014. "The Death of 'Gamers' and the Women Who 'Killed' Them." *Ars Technica*, August 28.

Juul, Jesper. 2010. *A Casual Revolution: Reinventing Video Games and Their Players.* Cambridge, MA: MIT Press.

Kaceytron. 2014. "I am professional girl gamer Kaceytron, AMA." *Reddit*, October 4.

Kafai, Yasmine B., Carrie Heeter, Jill Denner, and Jennifer Y. Sun, eds. 2008. *Beyond Barbie and "Mortal Kombat": New Perspectives on Gender and Gaming.* Cambridge, MA: MIT Press.

Kain, Erik. 2012. "Generic *BioShock Infinite* Box Art Fails to Impress." *Forbes*, December 2.

———. 2014. "GamerGate: A Closer Look at the Controversy Sweeping Video Games." *Forbes*, September 4.

Kapalka, Jason. 2006. "10 Ways to Make a BAD Casual Game." *Casual Connect* (Summer).

Kapp, Karl M. 2012. *The Gamification of Learning and Instruction: Game-Based Methods and Strategies for Training and Education.* Malden, MA: Wiley.

kataiki. 2014. "Harvest Moon: Friends of Mineral Town True Love Edition." *Tumblr*, September 7.

Kelly, R. Todd. 2013. "The Masculine Mystique." *Daily Beast*, October 20.

Kenna W. 2013. "Zelda Starring Zelda: The Story." *Kenna Stuff*, March 15.

Kennedy, Helen W. 2002. "Lara Croft: Feminist Icon or Virtual Bimbo? On the Limits of Textual Analysis." *Game Studies* 2 (2).

Kevar. 2009. "GLBT discrimination in forums? Message 180. *Star Wars: The Old Republic Community.*

Khazan, Olga. 2014. "Rise of the Feminist Tinder-Creep Busting Vigilante." *Atlantic*, October 27.

Kimmel, Michael. 2008. *Guyland: The Perilous World Where Boys Become Men.* New York: HarperCollins.

————. 2013. *Angry White Men: American Masculinity at the End of an Era.* New York: Nation Books.

KingofAsia. 2013. "Its so weird why do 99% of girls play support." *GameFAQs,* January 10.

Knobel, Michele, and Colin Lankshear. 2007. "Online Memes, Affinities, and Cultural Production." In *A New Literacies Sampler,* edited by Michele Knobel and Colin Lankshear, 199–228. New York: Peter Lang.

Kohler, Chris. 2008. "Cliffy B: *Gears of War 2* More 'Girlfriend-Friendly.'" *Wired,* May 16.

Krahulik, Mike. 2010. "Tragedy Is When I Cut My Finger." *Penny Arcade,* 13 August.

————. 2011. "Dickwolves." *Penny Arcade,* January 29.

Kubik, Erica. 2012. "Masters of Technology: Defining and Theorizing the Hardcore/Casual Dichotomy in Video Game Culture." In *Cyberfeminism 2.0,* edited by Radhika Gajjala and Yeon Ju Oh, 135–52. New York: Peter Lang.

Kuchera, Ben. 2011. "*Dragon Age II*'s Gay Character Controversial with Straight, Gay Gamers." *Ars Technica,* March 29.

Kücklich, Julian. 2005. "Precarious Playbour: Modders and the Digital Games Industry." *Fibreculture Journal,* no. 5.

Lehdonvirta, Mika, Yosuke Nagashima, Vili Lehdonvirta, and Akira Baba. 2012. "The Stoic Male: How Avatar Gender Affects Help-Seeking Behavior in an Online Game." *Games and Culture* 7 (1): 29–47.

Lehdonvirta, Vili. 2010. "Virtual Worlds Don't Exist: Questioning the Dichotomous Approach in MMO Studies." *Game Studies* 10 (1).

Lejack, Yannick. 2012. "'Why is the player on the side of killing?': An Interview with the Writer of *Far Cry 3.*" *Kill Screen,* December 12.

Lewis, Helen. 2012a. "*Gamers Against Bigotry* Is Hacked . . . By Gamers in Favour of Bigotry." *New Statesman,* July 24.

————. 2012b. "This Is What Online Harassment Looks Like." *New Statesman,* July 6.

Lewis, Matt K. 2015. "What's Behind the 'Cuckservative' Slur? (NSFW)." *Daily Caller,* July 23.

Lin, Holin. 2008. "Body, Space, and Gendered Gaming Experiences: A Cultural Geography of Homes, Cybercafés, and Dormatories." In Kafai et al. 2008, 67–82.

Lindell. 2012. "There Are No Girls on the Internet." *Know Your Meme,* August 18.

Loeb, Steven. 2013. "Women in Gaming: Ignored or Victims of Sexism." *Vator News,* May 6.

LordByrondathird. 2009. "GLBT discrimination in forums?" (message 15). *Star Wars: The Old Republic Community*.

MacCallum-Stewart, Esther. 2008. "Real Boys Carry Girly Epics: Normalising Gender Bending in Online Games." *Eludamos: Journal for Computer Game Culture* 2 (1): 27–40.

———. 2014. "'Take that, bitches!': Refiguring Lara Croft in Feminist Game Narratives." *Game Studies* 14 (2).

Maffetone, Elizabeth. 2013. "'People just don't know their place anymore': Utopia and Xenophobia in *BioShock Infinite*." Paper presented at Imagining Alternatives: A Graduate Symposium on Speculative Fictions, University of Illinois, Urbana, October 18.

Manjoo, Farhad. 2012. "Stop Calling Me a Troll: Just Because You Disagree with Me Doesn't Mean I Am One." *Slate*, December 5.

Matulef, Jeffrey. 2012. "*Far Cry 3*'s Writer Argues Critics Largely Missed the Point of the Game." *Eurogamer*, December 18.

Mayo, Marilyn. 2015. "White Supremacists Relish 'Cuckservative' Controversy." *Anti-Defamation League*, August 11.

McDonough, Katie. 2014. "Elisabeth Hasselbeck: Are Feminists and Wussy Men a Threat to National Security?" *Salon*, January 17.

McEwan, Melissa. 2010. "Survivors Are So Sensitive." *Shakesville*, August 13.

McGonigal, Jane. 2008. "Why *I Love Bees*: A Case Study in Collective Intelligence Gaming." In *The Ecology of Games: Connecting Youth, Games, and Learning*, edited by Katie Salen, 199–228. Cambridge, MA: MIT Press.

"The Men's Rights Movement: Why It Is So Controversial?" 2015. *The Week*, February 19.

Messner, Michael A. 2000. "Barbie Girls versus Sea Monsters: Children Constructing Gender." *Gender and Society* 14 (6): 765–84.

Meyer, Robert, and Michael Cukier. 2006. "Assessing the Attack Threat Due to IRC Channels." *Proceedings of the International Conference on Dependable Systems and Networks*, 467–72.

Mika, Mike. 2013. "Why I Hacked *Donkey Kong* for My Daughter." *Wired*, March 11.

Millie A. 2010. "Rape Is Hilarious, Part 53 in an Ongoing Series." *Shakesville*, August 12.

Morias, Betsy. 2013. "The Unfunniest Joke in Technology." *New Yorker*, September 9.

MostlyBiscuit. 2015. "Out of Character: An Interview with Twitch Streamer Kaceytron." *FemHype*, February 20.

Mother Jones News Team. 2014. "Women Harassed Out of Their Homes. Mass

Shooting Threats. How #Gamergate Morphed into a Monster." *Mother Jones*, October 16.

Murphy, Meghan. 2013. "The Rise of Hipster Sexism." *Herizons* (Summer).

Mystery. 2007. *The Mystery Method: How to Get Beautiful Women into Bed*. New York: St. Martin's Press.

Nakamura, Lisa. 2002. *Cybertypes: Race, Ethnicity, and Identity on the Internet*. New York: Routledge.

———. 2008. *Digitizing Race: Visual Cultures of the Internet*. Minneapolis: University of Minnesota Press.

Nebulae. 2012. "Why do girls play healers in most cases?" *MMO Champion* (February).

nerdonator. 2013. "Is Kaceytron trolling?" *Reddit*, November 23.

NewsThisSecond. 2016. "Trump: I'm Not a Politician, Thank Goodness" (video). *YouTube*, August 21.

Ngak, Chanda. 2013. "E3 Audience Offended by 'Rape Joke' at Microsoft Xbox One Event." *CBS News*, June 11.

Nitsche, Michael. 2011. "Machinima as Media." In *The Machinima Reader*, edited by Henry Lowood and Michael Nitsche, 113–26. Cambridge, MA: MIT Press.

"No right answer: is Anita Sarkeesian wrong?" 2014. *Escapist*, January 3.

Nuwer, Hank, ed. 2004. *The Hazing Reader*. Bloomington: Indiana University Press.

Nuzzi, Olivia. 2016. "How Pepe the Frog Became a Nazi Trump Supporter and Alt-Right Symbol." *Daily Beast*, May 26.

O'Leary, Amy. 2012. "In Virtual Play, Sex Harassment Is All Too Real." *New York Times*, August 1.

OKCThrowaway22221. 2014. "As a guy, I wanted to know what it was like to be a woman on a dating site, so I set up a fake profile and the end result was not something I was expecting (long)." *Reddit*, January 8.

Ori. 2009. "Girls Play Healers." *DiscoPriest*, October 29.

Paladinjoe. 2012. "Are most healers female?" *World of Warcraft Forums*, February 24.

Pascoe, C. J. 2007. *Dude, You're a Fag: Masculinity and Sexuality in High School*. Berkeley: University of California Press.

Payne, Matthew Thomas. 2016. *Playing War: Military Video Games after 9/11*. New York: New York University Press.

Peacock, Joe. 2012. "Booth Babes Need Not Apply." *Geek Out!*, July 24.

Pearson, Dan. 2013. "EA, BioWare Fire-Fighting Reactions to SWtOR's 'Gay Ghetto' Planet." *Games Industry Biz*, January 15.

Phillips, Whitney. 2013. "Ethnography of Trolling: Workarounds, Discipline-

Jumping, and Ethical Pitfalls (Part 1 of 3)." *Ethnography Matters*, January 8.

pleaseTWITCHdontMUTEem. 2014. "Kaceytron's Donations" (video). *YouTube*, November 20.

Plunkett, Luke. 2012. "Awful Things Happen When You Try to Make a Video about Video Game Stereotypes." *Kotaku*, June 12.

Poe, Nathan. 2015. "Poe's Law." *Christian Forums*, August 10.

Polo, Susana. 2012. "On the 'Fake' Geek Girl." *Mary Sue*, March 27.

Potok, Mark, and Evelyn Schlatter. 2012. "Men's Rights Movement Spreads False Claims about Women." *Southern Poverty Law Center*, March 1.

punkniner. 2009a. "GLBT discrimination in forums?" (message 46). *Star Wars: The Old Republic Community*.

————. 2009b. "GLBT discrimination in forums?" (message 76). *Star Wars: The Old Republic Community*.

Quart, Alissa. 2012. "The Age of Hipster Sexism." *NYMag*, October 30.

Rae, Simon. 2001. "C&IT in the Humanities." In *Contemporary Themes in Humanities Higher Education*, edited by E. A. Chambers, 125–52. Dordrecht: Kluwer Academic.

Raja, Tasneem. 2012. "'Gangbang Interviews' and 'Bikini Shots': Silicon Valley's Brogrammer Problem." *Mother Jones*, April 26.

Rath, Robert. 2013. "*Far Cry 3*'s Cindra Is Straight from the Freakshow." *Escapist*, February 28.

Reeves, Byron, and J. Leighton Reed. 2009. *Total Engagement*. Cambridge, MA: Harvard Business School Press.

Rheingold, Howard. 1993. *The Virtual Communities: Homesteading on the Electronic Frontier*. Reading, MA: Addison-Wesley.

Rich, Adrienne. 1980. "Compulsory Heterosexuality and Lesbian Existence." *Signs* 5 (4): 631–60.

Rubin, Gayle. 2011. "The Traffic in Women: Notes on the 'Political Economy' of Sex." In *Deviations: A Gayle Rubin Reader*, 1–32. Durham, NC: Duke University Press.

"Rules of Conduct." 2011. *Star Wars: The Old Republic Community*.

"The Rules of the Internet." 2007. *4chan*, Februrary 15.

Rundle, Michael. 2012. "*Borderlands 2*: Gearbox Studios Developer Infuriates Gamers with 'Girlfriend Mode' Comment." *Huffington Post UK*, August 13.

"The R-Word." 2012. *Escapist*, June 25.

"Safety and Security." 2013. *PAX Prime*, September 19.

Salmon, Catherine, and Donald Symons. 2003. *Warrior Lovers: Erotic Fiction, Evolution and Female Sexuality*. New Haven, CT: Yale University Press.

Salter, Anastasia, and Bridget Blodgett. 2012. "Hypermasculinity and Dickwolves: The Contentious Role of Women in the New Gaming Public." *Journal of Broadcasting and Electronic Media* 56 (3): 401–16.

Sarah. 2013. "A Damsel in Progress: Analyzing *BioShock Infinite*'s Elizabeth." *About-Face*, April 29.

Sarkeesian, Anita (feministfrequency). 2013a. "Damsel in Distress—Part I: Tropes vs Women in Video Games" (video). *YouTube*, March 7.

———. 2013b. "Damsel in Distress—Part II: Tropes vs Women in Video Games" (video). *YouTube*, May 28.

———. 2012a. "Anita Sarkeesian at TEDxWomen." *TEDxWomen*, December 4.

———. 2012b. "Harassment, Misogyny, and Silencing on YouTube." *Feminist Frequency*, June 7.

———. 2012c. "Harassment via Wikipedia Vandalism." *Feminist Frequency*, June 10.

———. 2012d. "Image Based Harassment and Visual Misogyny." *Feminist Frequency*, July 1.

———. 2012e. "Tropes vs. Women in Video Games." *Kickstarter*, June 16.

Schiesel, Seth. 2006. "Welcome to the Dollhouse." *New York Times*, May 7.

Scullion, Chris. 2013. "Xbox One 'Employs Advanced Troll Detection.'" *Computer and Video Games*, July 3.

Serwer, Adam, and Katie J. M. Baker. 2015. "How Men's Rights Leader Paul Elam Turned Being a Deadbeat Dad into a Moneymaking Movement." *BuzzFeed*, February 6.

Shariatmadari, David. 2016. "'Virtue-Signalling'—The Putdown That Has Passed Its Sell-By Date." *Guardian*, January 20.

Shaw, Adrienne. 2009. "Putting the Gay in Games: Cultural Production and GLBT Content in Video Games." *Games and Culture* 4 (3): 228–53.

Sheldon, Lee. 2012. *The Multiplayer Classroom: Designing Coursework as a Game*. Boston: Cengage Learning.

Sherle_Illios. 2009. "GLBT discrimination in forums?" (message 41). *Star Wars: The Old Republic Community*.

Shifman, Limon. 2014. *Memes in Digital Culture*. Cambridge, MA: MIT Press.

Singal, Jesse. 2016. "Explaining the Drama at the Internet's Largest Donald Trump Community." *New York Magazine*, June 24.

Sliwinski, Alexander. 2009. "BioWare's Old Republic Policy on Homosexuality Reconsidered." *Joystiq*, April 29.

Social Justice Bread. 2014. "#GamerOverGate." *Storify*.

SorionHex. 2013. "Why do girls always play support??" *League of Legends Forums*, April 5.

Speel, Hans-Cees. 1996. "Memetics: On a Conceptual Framework for Cultural

Evolution." In *The Evolution of Complexity*, edited by Francis Heylighen and Diederik Aerts. Dordrecht: Kluwer.

Squire, Kurt. 2011. *Video Games and Learning: Teaching and Participatory Culture in the Digital Age*. New York: Teachers College Press.

Stanfill, Mel. 2010. "Doing Fandom, (Mis)doing Whiteness: Heteronormativity, Racialization, and the Discursive Construction of Fandom." *Transformative Works and Cultures*, no. 8.

Stanfill, Mel, and Megan Condis. 2014. "Fandom and/as Labor." *Transformative Works and Cultures*, no. 15.

Stanton, Courtney. 2011a. "Here Is a Project: Troll! Data! Analysis!" *Super Opinionated*, February 8.

Stanton, Courtney. 2011b. "Here Is a Shirt: Dickwolves Survivor's Guild." *Super Opinionated*, February 2.

Sterling, Jim. 2012a. "*Far Cry 3*: The Creative Failure of Industry 'Commentary.'" *Destructoid*, December 18.

———. 2012b. "Jimquisition: Dumbing Down for the Filthy Casuals" (video). *Escapist*, December 10.

———. 2012c. "Jimquisition: Fake Nerd Girls" (video). *Escapist*, November 19.

Stone, Rosanne Allucquére. 2000. "Will the Real Body Please Stand Up? Boundary Stories about Virtual Cultures." In *The Cybercultures Reader*, edited by David Bell and Barbara M. Kennedy, 504–28. New York: Routledge.

Strauss, Neil. 2005. *The Game: Penetrating the Secret Society of Pickup Artists*. New York: HarperCollins.

———. 2007. *The Rules of the Game*. New York: HarperCollins.

Sundén, Jenny. 2003. *Material Virtualities: Approaching Online Textual Embodiment*. New York: Peter Lang.

Taiso. 2015. "Is Kaceytron for real or not?" *Neo-Geo Forums*, March 20.

Takahashi, Dean. 2016. "E3 Reels in 70,300 to Gaming's Biggest Tradeshow in North America." *Venture Beat*, June 16.

Tassi, Paul. 2012. "Why *Far Cry 3* Is Misunderstood." *Forbes Tech*, December 26.

Taylor, Brian. 2011. "Save Aeris: How Can We Be Moved by the Fate of Aeris Gainsborough (Kill Screen)." *BT Photographer*, September 4.

Taylor, T. L. 2012. *Raising the Stakes: E-Sports and the Professionalization of Computer Gaming*. Cambridge, MA: MIT Press.

Tepper, Michele. 1997. "Usenet Communities and the Cultural Politics of Information." In *Internet Culture*, edited by David Porter, 39–54. New York: Routledge.

Their, Dave. 2012. "Racism in *Far Cry 3*." *Forbes Tech*, December 10.

Thorn, Clarisse, and Julian Dibbell. 2012. *Violation: Rape in Gaming*. Seattle: CreateSpace Independent Publishing Platform.

Thurlow, C. 2001. "Naming the 'Outsider Within': Homophobic Pejoratives and the Verbal Abuse of Lesbian, Gay and Bisexual High-School Pupils." *Journal of Adolescence* 24:25–38.

Totilo, Stephen. 2009. "Nintendo Boasts 9 Million Player Advantage among Female Console Gamers." *Kotaku*, November 25.

———. 2014. "In Recent Days I've Been Asked Several Times." *Kotaku*, August 20.

Turgeman-Goldschmidt, Orly. 2005. "Hackers' Accounts: Hacking as Social Entertainment." *Social Science Computer Review* 23 (1): 8–23.

Turkle, Sherry. 1995. *Life on the Screen: Identity in the Age of the Internet*. New York: Simon & Schuster.

Turner, Fred. 2008. *From Counterculture to Cyberculture: Steward Brand, the Whole Earth Network, and the Rise of Digital Utopianism*. Chicago: University of Chicago Press.

Tuttle, Ian. 2016. "The Racist Moral Rot at the Heart of the Alt-Right." *National Review*, April 5.

Tweten, Alexandra. 2014. "Why I Created *Bye Felipe*." *Ms. Magazine Blog*, October 31.

Valizadeh, Roosh. 2014. "ROK Is Looking to Hire a GamerGate Correspondent." *Return of Kings*, October 21.

———. 2015. "How to Stop Rape." *Roosh V*, February 16.

Vanderhoef, John. 2013. "Casual Threats: The Feminization of Video Games." *Ada*, no. 2.

Viser, Matt. 2016. "Donald Trump Relies on a Simple Phrase: 'Believe Me.'" *Boston Globe*, May 24.

Wagner, Kyle. 2014. "The Future of the Culture Wars Is Here, and It's Gamergate." *Deadspin*, October 14.

Walker, John. 2012. "*Far Cry 3*'s Jeffrey Yohalem on Racism, Torture, and Satire." *Rock Paper Shotgun*, December 19.

Wang, Morten. 1998. "The Troller's FAQ." *Morten's Collection of Texts*, August 15.

Ward, Mark. 2006. "Gay Rights Win in *Warcraft* World." *BBC News*, February 13.

Warner, Michael. 1993. Introduction to *Fear of a Queer Planet: Queer Politics and Social Theory*, edited by Michael Warner, vii–xxxi. Minneapolis: University of Minnesota Press.

Warzel, Charlie. 2016. "Twitter Permanently Suspends Conservative Writer Milo Yiannopoulos." *BuzzFeed*, July 20.

Weil, Rachel Simone. 2013. "NES ROM Hacks and Discourses on Gender Anxieties." *No Bad Memories*, March 23.

Werbach, Kevin. 2012. *For the Win: How Game Thinking Can Revolutionize Your Business*. Philadelphia, PA: Warton Digital Press.

Wirman, Hanna. 2014. "Princess Peach Loves Your Enemies, Too." In *Game Love: Essays on Play and Affection*, edited by Jessica Enevold and Esther MacCallum-Stewart, 131–48. Jefferson, NC: McFarland.

Wofford, Taylor. 2014. "Is GamerGate about Media Ethics or Harassing Women? Harassment, the Data Shows." *Newsweek*, October 25.

Wysocki, Matthew, and Matthew Schandler. 2013. "Would You Kindly? *BioShock* and the Question of Control." In *Ctrl-Alt-Play: Essays on Control in Video Gaming*, edited by Matthew Wysocki, 196–207. Jefferson, NC: McFarland.

Yee, Nick. 2005. "*WoW* Character Class Demographics." *Daedelus Project*, July 28.

———. 2008. "Maps of Digital Desires: Exploring the Topography of Gender and Play in Online Games." In Kafai et al. 2008, 83–96.

Yee, Nick, Nicolas Ducheneaut, Mike Yao, and Les Nelson. 2011. "Do Men Heal More When in Drag? Conflicting Identity Cues between User and Avatar." In *Proceedings of the CHE*, May 7–12.

Zelenko, Michael. 2015. "A Brilliant Tinder Hack Made Hundreds of Bros Unwittingly Flirt with Each Other." *Verge*, March 25.

INDEX